POLITICIANS AND EDUCATION POLICY

Based on an in-depth case study, this book reveals how politicians, as policy makers, conceptualise, develop and initiate large-scale education system reform and why it matters for whole system school improvement.

Governments all over the world are spending increasing time, money and effort on improving school systems but the evidence suggests that few of them are getting it right. There is much research devoted to educational strategies, policies, reform initiatives and outcomes. However, what is often missing is a generally agreed set of policies or principles which Ministers can draw on as a guiding framework. This book shows how political context impacts the development of education policy and reveals the critical and dynamic relationship between politics, policy and process. This book gives new insights into politicians as leaders in large-scale education system reform, distils lessons and identifies three practical strategic frameworks which provide new ways of understanding and engaging in whole system reform.

Offering unique "insider" insights from an Education Minister, their staff, public servants and key stakeholders, this book is written for all politicians, policy makers and educators involved in school improvement, as well as students of educational leadership and policy.

Sheridan Dudley is an Honorary Senior Lecturer, School of Education, University of NSW, Australia, and was Company Secretary of the International Congress for School Effectiveness and Improvement (ICSEI). Dudley was Chief of Staff to the NSW Minister for Education, has lectured at several Australian universities and was Visiting Associate Professor at Wuhan Iron and Steel University.

POLITICIANS AND EDUCATION POLICY

Why It Matters for Whole System Improvement

Sheridan Dudley

Designed cover image: © Getty Images

First published 2025
by Routledge
4 Park Square, Milton Park, Abingdon, Oxon OX14 4RN

and by Routledge
605 Third Avenue, New York, NY 10158

Routledge is an imprint of the Taylor & Francis Group, an informa business

© 2025 Sheridan Dudley

The right of Sheridan Dudley to be identified as author of this work has been asserted in accordance with sections 77 and 78 of the Copyright, Designs and Patents Act 1988.

All rights reserved. No part of this book may be reprinted or reproduced or utilised in any form or by any electronic, mechanical, or other means, now known or hereafter invented, including photocopying and recording, or in any information storage or retrieval system, without permission in writing from the publishers.

Trademark notice: Product or corporate names may be trademarks or registered trademarks, and are used only for identification and explanation without intent to infringe.

British Library Cataloguing-in-Publication Data
A catalogue record for this book is available from the British Library

ISBN: 978-1-032-84842-6 (hbk)
ISBN: 978-1-032-84841-9 (pbk)
ISBN: 978-1-003-51526-5 (ebk)

DOI: 10.4324/9781003515265

Typeset in Times New Roman
by KnowledgeWorks Global Ltd.

CONTENTS

Foreword by Professor Emeritus David Hopkins   viii
Acknowledgements   xi
About the author   xii

PART I
Challenges for politicians as policy makers in education system reform   1

1 Politicians as policy makers: The "black box" of whole system reform   3

2 Whole system improvement and the problem for governments   9

   Three issues for governments in whole system improvement 9
   The role of politicians in policy development 14
   What is the system in large-scale system reform? 17
   The role of Ministers in developing large-scale education system reform 20

PART II
Politics, power and ideology: The development of *Local Schools, Local Decisions*   25

3   Starting the reform process: Conceptualising the LSLD reform   27

The historical and political education reform context 27
Developing a new education reform agenda in NSW 29
Insights from stakeholders 33
Analytical Reflection 35

4   Encountering and aligning competing reform goals   39

Encountering competing reform goals 39
The turning point: the "Better Schools" Presentation 45
Aligning the reform goals and defining the outcomes 47
Analytical Reflection 53

5   Consultation and engagement: Building support and managing opposition   58

The formal consultation context 59
Engaging and consulting with education stakeholders 60
Engaging with politicians and government stakeholders 71
Analytical Reflection 73

6   From policy discourse and data to policy text and the announcement of LSLD   79

The political context of the LSLD policy announcement 80
Determining the policy 81
Creating the policy documents 88
The announcement of LSLD 92
Perspectives on LSLD 93
Analytical Reflection 97

PART III
Politics, policy, processes and people in educational change   103

7   Understanding the role of politicians as policy makers   105

Theme 1: The importance of the political context 107
Theme 2: Engagement with key education stakeholders 109

Theme 3: The Minister's relationship with the Department 110
Theme 4: Staying close to schools 112
Theme 5: Using research evidence 114
Theme 6: Power and policy making 116
Theme 7: The relationship between policy and politics 118
Theme 8: The Minister's leadership role in policy making 119
Bringing the themes together: politics, policy, processes and people 120

8 Strategic frameworks and guiding principles for whole system improvement   122

Framework 1: The "Policy Process Bow Tie" 123
Framework 2: The Education Policy and Engagement System 127
Framework 3: Whole System Reform Policy Development 129
Guiding principles for policy development for politicians, policy makers, stakeholders, practitioners and researchers 132
Concluding Reflection: Why it matters for whole system school improvement 134

Appendix: Local Schools, Local Decisions: Fact Sheets	*136*
References	*142*
Index	*151*

FOREWORD

by Professor Emeritus David Hopkins

This is certainly a propitious time for Sheridan Dudley to publish her excellent book *Politicians and Education Policy*! As *TIME* magazine noted on 28 December 2023, "2024 is not just *an* election year. It's perhaps *the* election year". Almost half the world's population went to the polls in 2024, with further elections in 2025, and although education is not the major issue in every jurisdiction, education policy will inevitably be the focus of debate globally over the coming years more than ever before. I will explain briefly in this Foreword why Sheridan Dudley's book has such a significant contribution to make to this debate.

The publication of *Politicians and Education Policy* comes at a time when we, as a global educational community, have learned an increasing amount about large-scale educational change. Some will recall that in the 1980s, following the publication of *Fifteen Thousand Hours* (Rutter et al., 1979) that first articulated the characteristics of effective schools, the school improvement movement emerged and developed. In the same way, over the past 20 years, data from the OECD's *Programme for International Student Assessment* (PISA) has laid the basis for identifying the features of effective educational systems and ways to improve them.

There is however a danger, as Sheridan Dudley points out, that these characteristics will be over-simplified and presented in a reductionist way, like a list of ingredients rather than a recipe for innovative reform. Others agree. Michael Fullan (2011) in outlining his "wrong drivers for whole system reform" critiques approaches that emphasise accountability rather than capacity building, and fragmented rather than systemic policies. Similarly, it is Pasi Sahlberg (2012) who warns us of the ubiquitous GERM virus that manifests itself in low-risk ways of reaching learning goals and test-based accountability systems. Both of these policies may under some conditions raise standards minimally in the short term, but they will also ensure that systems which employ them will rapidly regress to the mean or worse.

For these reasons, among others, we have been advocating an approach to system reform that vertically links together the various levels of the system and horizontally integrates key policy initiatives that focus unrelentingly on the instructional core. To reiterate the four crucial points (Hopkins, 2024; Hopkins & Mackay, 2024):

- First, single reforms do not work, it is only clusters of linked policy initiatives that will provide the necessary traction.
- Second, the drivers need to build capacity for equity as well as raising standards for excellence.
- Third, it is system leadership that drives implementation and adapts policies to context.
- Fourth, the generation and sustaining of an overarching narrative at all levels that links moral purpose to strategic action is mandatory.

But even this more comprehensive approach is, as Sheridan Dudley points out, insufficient to reliably raise standards, change behaviours and sustain them over time. It is in explaining this conundrum that her book has so much value and makes such a significant contribution.

Sheridan Dudley is one of those rare educators who has located their professional practice and reflection in the middle of that triangle bounded by the vertices of schools, research and policy. It is this self-conscious professional positioning that has enabled her to draw such important insights.

In March 2011, Sheridan Dudley took up the role of Chief of Staff to the new Minister for Education in New South Wales (NSW), Adrian Piccoli. For the following five years, she supported and managed his radical and innovative approach to educational policy making and implementation. Perhaps the most significant of these was *Local Schools, Local Decisions* (LSLD). LSLD was a large-scale education system reform that had a significant impact on the governance, funding and decision-making authority of all government schools. To many, this policy represented potentially the greatest change ever to school governance and decision-making in NSW public education. LSLD attempted to balance two key ideas which reflect our own approach to system reform noted above – give principals and teachers more authority to direct their resources towards improving student outcomes, whilst at the same time, retaining the strengths of belonging to a strong, state-wide government education system.

Sometime later it was LSLD that became the focus of Sheridan Dudley's Doctoral research. Here she undertook a detailed, qualitative case study of the processes through which Minister Piccoli, in his role as a policy maker, conceptualised and developed the LSLD initiative. It was this impressive research study that lays the basis for this book.

The research that underpins *Politicians and Education Policy* is thoroughly and intelligently conducted, so the conclusions are sound. The real value of the book however lies in the final two chapters, where Sheridan Dudley moves beyond her original research questions and uses her assiduously collected and analysed data to generate a series of themes and frameworks that Ministers should use in policy development and implementation. The details are in the chapters that follow, so I will not rehearse them here. But what is so impressive is that she has generated a policy development and implementation framework that integrates in a realistic way a series of proposals that value, balance and integrate the perspectives of practice, research and policy that form the axes of the triangle mentioned above.

This now takes me back to my opening comments regarding election years. The debates on educational policy in the various systems that I have been following have been conducted at a superficial level. At best, there is an implicit assumption that merely outlining a policy will lead to action and the outcomes that advocates claim for it. Sheridan Dudley deftly exposes this charade by unpacking in forensic detail the intricate but necessary implementation process that Ministers need to follow if a policy, however well-conceived, is to have a positive impact. It is here where the real value of Sheridan Dudley's book lies and where the debate on educational policy in election years and beyond should be conducted. If the lessons of *Politicians and Education Policy* are followed, then we will have a much better chance of ensuring that both excellence and equity are achieved in our global education systems.

References

Fullan, M. (2011). *Choosing the wrong drivers for whole system reform*. CSE seminar series, paper no. 204, May, Centre for Strategic Education.

Hopkins, D. (2024). *Unleashing greatness – A strategy for school improvement*. John Catt Educational.

Hopkins, D., & Mackay, A. (2024). Achieving equity through excellence in the world's education systems. *CSE occasional paper series*, July, Centre for Strategic Education.

Rutter, M., Maughan, B., Mortimore, P., Ouston, J., with Smith, A. (1979). *Fifteen thousand hours*. Open Books.

Sahlberg, P. (2012). *Global educational reform movement is here!* https://pasisahlberg.com/global-educational-reform-movement-is-here/

ACKNOWLEDGEMENTS

My heartfelt gratitude goes to Adrian Piccoli, former NSW Minister for Education, whom I had the privilege of serving as Chief of Staff for five years. Adrian always encouraged my research and generously shared his own writings with me, from which I have quoted extensively with his permission. This book could not have been undertaken without his support.

This book draws significantly from, and then develops and expands on, my doctoral thesis at the University of NSW (Dudley, 2023). My deepest thanks and appreciation go to Associate Professor Richard Niesche and Emeritus Professor Colin Evers for their warm and thoughtful guidance that shaped my journey from a storyteller writing a memoir, to a scholar writing a research report, and then encouraged and supported me to write this book.

Special thanks go to my colleagues at the International Congress for School Effectiveness and Improvement (ICSEI) who have inspired, supported and encouraged me and who have given me a wealth of valuable international perspectives on whole system reform and school improvement. In particular, I would like to thank Professor Andy Hargreaves who introduced me into ICSEI and encouraged me to undertake my doctorate, as well as Professor David Hopkins, who gave me wise advice on broadening and deepening my post-doctoral research and generously provided the Foreword for this book.

The data sources for this book include publicly available documents such as discussion papers and policy documents, as well as my personal contemporaneous notebooks, Memoir Notes written by the Minister and interviews with the Minister, Minister's Office staff and key education stakeholders who were participants in the process, which are all used with their permission. Copyright documents from the NSW Department of Education are also used with permission from the Department.

ABOUT THE AUTHOR

Dr Sheridan Dudley is an Honorary Senior Lecturer, School of Education, at UNSW.

She has over 40 years' experience in education as an academic, policy maker and leader in the government and not-for-profit sectors. She was Chief of Staff to the NSW Minister for Education, Adrian Piccoli for five years, while he introduced 19 large-scale system reforms, and she has provided education policy advice to Premiers in NSW and Victoria.

She has been a Visiting Associate Professor at Wuhan Iron and Steel University, lectured at several Australian universities and was chief executive of KU Children's Services, then Australia's largest not-for-profit provider of early childhood education and care.

She has a Doctor of Education from UNSW, a Masters of Administration (public policy and administration) from Monash University and Law and Arts degrees from the University of Melbourne. Her research interests are in the politics of education and education policy in large-scale system reform.

PART I
Challenges for politicians as policy makers in education system reform

PART I

1
POLITICIANS AS POLICY MAKERS

The "black box" of whole system reform

> It was clear to me that the system was holding us back from making major school improvements and delivering better outcomes for students. So, my starting point as the Minister for Education in NSW is that every decision we make, every policy, every funding allocation, must be judged against the yardstick of: "How does this improve the education of our students?"
>
> (Adrian Piccoli)

For the past 60 years, large-scale education system reforms, aimed at improving systems, policies and outcomes for students, have been developed, implemented and researched around the world. Since the 1980s, this has been a major preoccupation of governments as many developed nations realised their education systems would not be able to lead the way in dealing with the economic, technological and social transformations that were developing globally. At the same time, the stakes of education reform have continued to rise. The growing use and profile of international student assessment data, especially the Programme for International Student Assessment (PISA), has increasingly influenced national education policies in a number of countries as educational success is viewed as a proxy for economic competitiveness and a lower-than-desired PISA result can therefore affect a nation's reputation and standing internationally.

Over the past 20 years, governments have therefore been investing increasing amounts of time, effort and money in large-scale system reforms. These have affected thousands of schools, impacted on more than 200 million students in Organisation for Economic Co-operation and Development (OECD) countries, and cost billions of dollars (OECD, 2015). However, despite the immense effort, investment and research, whole system improvement – where the vast majority of schools improve – continues to remain elusive in many education systems

(Fullan, 2016a), while student performance is actually declining in a number of countries.

The problem for governments is that they are spending increasing amounts of effort and money on large-scale system reforms, and the stakes of their involvement in it are rising. However, the evidence suggests that few of them are getting it right and that "more and more people, including politicians, are becoming convinced that the policy drivers that they have favoured for the past two decades ... do not bring about system change...[and] are actually propelling us backwards" (Fullan & Gallagher, 2020, p. 21).

These increasing concerns over the failure of large-scale education system reform to deliver the desired results of whole system school improvement have led to considerable research on educational strategies, policies, reform initiatives and outcomes in a large number of countries. There has also been a range of international reports and studies which increasingly focus on case studies of both schools and reforms across entire national and state education systems[1]. The OECD (2015) claims that this has increased understanding of school reform and led to a general consensus around what works.

However, while the findings of these studies are not inconsistent, what stands out is that they do not identify any generally agreed set of policies or principles upon which governments might draw in developing large-scale system reforms. Indeed, Hopkins et al. (2014), who develop their own list of ten features of high-performing national systems, somewhat ironically caution that this type of research is like creating a list of ingredients rather than a recipe, and that educational systems and the necessary levers for systemic reform will vary greatly by national systemic context.

This raises challenges for governments as, despite general agreement that politicians are integral to public policy development (Hoppe, 2018; Virani, 2019), there is little clear guidance that they might use in conceptualising, developing and initiating large-scale education system reform in the political contexts within which they operate. There is also a general consensus that, despite its importance, very little systematic research actually exists on the politics of reform (Bruns & Schneider, 2016). Particular areas where research is lacking relate to the unique constraints and pressures under which governments and politicians operate (Levin, 2009) and to the role of actors, politics and what parts of the political processes of reform went well or poorly, which are "still largely a 'black box'" (Busemeyer & Trampusch, 2011, p. 432)[2]. A finer-grained knowledge of how to manage system reform over time is therefore required and successful school and system improvement will need "ever more practical – and more applied – research" (Hopkins et al., 2014, p. 272).

One area where there is only very limited practical research is how politicians, in their role as policy makers, initiate and develop large-scale education system reforms. Apart from some memoirs by former Education Ministers, the voices of politicians in describing and analysing their roles in policy development and reform design, what might be learned from them and how this could assist education policy makers more generally, are almost entirely absent. Another area which appears to be completely missing from the research is any detailed study of the process of the development of a single large-scale education system reform policy in the political context of an Education Minister's office, which is informed not only by the insider perspectives of the minister and his/her staff but also by the senior public servants and the key education stakeholders who were insiders to the process.

The resulting problem for politicians as policy makers is that there are no firm right answers, no agreed processes or frameworks for undertaking large-scale education system reform and no "reform in a box" solution they can easily apply (Hopkins et al., 2014, p. 272). Ministers are therefore faced with a series of dilemmas and decisions as they design such reforms without a framework which they can use to guide them. This would be beneficial as most ministers arrive in office with a policy platform and some ideas but with not much knowledge about how to actually achieve lasting large-scale system reform that has impact, rather than just "putting lipstick on a pig".

This problem was immediately apparent to me in Australia when a new Liberal/Nationals [Conservative] Government was elected in the State of New South Wales (NSW) in March 2011. Adrian Piccoli was appointed as the Minister for Education, and at his invitation, I took up the role as his Chief of Staff[3] and resigned from my position as Chief Executive Officer of the largest and oldest not-for-profit provider of early childhood education and care services in Australia.

The Minister's portfolio comprised all education in NSW, from early childhood through school education including both government and non-government schools, vocational education and training, and university governance, as well as education standards, curriculum, assessment and teacher standards. It had a budget of AUD 12.2 billion (approximately one-quarter of the NSW State Government Budget) and included one of the largest public school education systems in the world (Sherington & Hughes, 2012) with 2,200 public schools, approximately 750,000 students and around 100,000 staff[4].

Despite having joined the worldwide trend of implementing large-scale system reform, Australia was still falling behind in international education comparisons. Between 2003 and 2009, the PISA results showed that Australia as a whole had declined in reading literacy, while NSW had slipped back about half a year against international standards and there was an increasing proportion of low-performing students (Thomson et al., 2010). To address this, between 2011 and 2016 Minister Piccoli introduced nineteen large-scale education system reforms which, taken together, constituted the most comprehensive reforms to education in NSW in a century (NSW Department of Education, 2017).

But the problem for the Minister and his Office was that there was no consensus about how to create successful whole system improvement and no generally accepted framework or model we could use to do it. In particular, while I knew that politicians are integral to public policy development, there was almost no research or guidance as to what they or their offices actually did, step-by-step, day-by-day, in developing policy – which meant making it up and learning as we went along.

My five years of experience in the Minister's Office during a period when so many major reforms were developed and implemented also brought home to me that, despite my long career as a key education stakeholder, as a senior public servant with experience in designing and implementing large-scale system reforms in a wide range of portfolios, as well as whole of government public sector reform, and as an academic specialising in public policy and administration, I had probably not engaged as collaboratively or productively with politicians and their offices as I might have done. On reflection, this was because neither they nor I had deep insight into what they did, what they needed and when they needed it, and because we did not have the conceptual and analytical frameworks available to ensure we were not "simply talking past one another" (Spillane, 2013, p. 39).

This book was therefore born out of my desire to play a part in addressing that gap in our knowledge by providing insights into how politicians develop large-scale education system reform policies. And my background both as a policy maker and an academic meant that I did not simply want to write a memoir about my experiences. Instead, I wanted to establish research-based evidence into the Minister's role in policy development and draw on it to identify practical strategic frameworks and distil some guiding principles which might assist politicians, as well as policy makers, stakeholders and researchers more broadly, to develop whole system reforms that could have an increased chance of successful outcomes for our students and our schools.

I therefore undertook a detailed, qualitative descriptive case study of the processes through which Minister Piccoli, in his role as a policy maker, conceptualised and developed the large-scale education system reform *Local Schools, Local Decisions* (LSLD) in its system and political contexts. LSLD was one of the first and most complex of the NSW education reforms during that period and had significant impacts on the governance, funding and decision-making authority of all 2,200 government schools, as well as on the Central Office of the Department, over the next ten years. LSLD balanced two important ideas – giving principals and teachers more authority to direct their resources towards improving student outcomes, whilst at the same time, retaining the strengths of belonging to a strong, state-wide government education system (Piccoli, 2014). It was a major focus of the policy work by the Minister and his Office during 2011 and was formally announced in March 2012, after almost a year in development, when it was described by Stephen Dinham (2012, p. 13) as "a policy document representing potentially the greatest change to school governance and decision-making in more than 160 years of public education in NSW".

I chose to study LSLD because, despite the scope and scale of the NSW education reforms during Piccoli's tenure as Education Minister, the number of studies on them in general, and of LSLD in particular, is very limited. Some studies mention the introduction of LSLD but do not discuss it in any detail[5], while other studies focus on industrial relations issues related to LSLD, such as teacher working conditions and union opposition[6]. Other research focuses on the impact of LSLD more broadly[7]; however, none of these considers the development of the policy. The most comprehensive review of LSLD is the formal evaluation undertaken by the Centre for Education Statistics and Evaluation (2018, 2020). It included a process evaluation that investigated the implementation of LSLD and an outcome evaluation focusing on the impact of the reform on school and student outcomes. However, it did not cover the process of the development of LSLD or the role of the Minister.

While these studies all add their own insights into LSLD, none of them takes a political perspective on the processes through which the LSLD reform was conceptualised and developed by the Minister for Education and our Office in the absence of any strategic framework or road map to guide us, nor do they provide insights into the politics of policy making, which is the focus of this book.

I have undertaken this research as a policy historian who was a "complete insider" to the policy development process in my role as Chief of Staff to the NSW Minister for Education, as well as having 30 years of senior executive-level public policy development and large-scale system reform experience. This positionality gives me the benefit of an epistemically privileged perspective on the events which I describe, document and analyse, as I was deeply immersed and embedded in the development of LSLD and the other reforms and I have detailed knowledge of my research subject. However, my insider positionality has other implications which are potentially problematic, such as subjectivity and verification bias. I have therefore taken a reflexive approach (Braun & Clarke, 2013) to myself as the researcher, by examining and consciously acknowledging the assumptions and preconceptions I bring into the research that might shape the outcomes.

In the case study, I have focused exclusively on the process of the development of the LSLD policy by the Minister for Education and his Office in the political context of government, up until its announcement. I did not evaluate whether its implementation was successful and was agnostic as to the quality and effectiveness of the reform. Nor did I consider the role of the broader public service or other organisations in the development of LSLD, except insofar as they intersected with the processes being undertaken by the Minister and his Office. In that regard, the case study might be seen as the view of system reform from *The West Wing* rather than that of the bureaucracy[8]. And to maintain a focus on gaining insights into the policy development process from the personal insider perspective of a Minister, each chapter commences with a quotation from Adrian Piccoli and his own words are extensively quoted in text boxes throughout this book.

My analysis of the case study builds on the small literature on the politics of education regarding the role of ministers, as well as on the extensive literature on large-scale education system reform and public policy development, to identify what was occurring at the overall level of politics and policy development, how it links to what we know about large-scale system reform, the politics of education, education policy development and systems theory, and what we can learn from it.

I then use this analysis to draw out eight overarching themes which provide new insights into the role of politicians as policy makers and the processes they use in conceptualising, developing and initiating large-scale education system reform policies. I build on these themes to develop three new practical strategic frameworks and ten guiding principles for all those engaged in the development of whole system reform. It is my hope that these might shape and focus the process of education policy development, so that politicians, practitioners, policy makers, key stakeholders and researchers are able to talk with, rather than past one another in designing effective policies for whole system school improvement.

Notes

1 For example, see Barber and Mourshed (2007), Fullan (2010), Hargreaves and Shirley (2012), Levin (2008), OECD (2015) and Sahlberg (2012).
2 See also, Bruns and Schneider (2016), Mourshed et al. (2010) and Shrestha et al. (2019).
3 The Chief of Staff is the head of a Minister's private office and is also known as the Principal Private Secretary in the United Kingdom.
4 In Australia, government schools are generally referred to as "public schools". Both terms will be used interchangeably in this book.
5 See Caldwell (2016) and Griffin (2013).
6 See Gavin (2019), Gavin and McGrath-Champ (2017), Gavin et al. (2022) and McGrath-Champ et al. (2019).
7 See Eacott et al. (2022), Gavin and Stacey (2022) and Hingston (2018).
8 *The West Wing* was an American political drama TV series, primarily set in the West Wing of the White House, where the Oval Office of the President and the offices of senior presidential staff are located. It follows a fictional President and his staff through their days as they work through particular legislative or political issues.

2
WHOLE SYSTEM IMPROVEMENT AND THE PROBLEM FOR GOVERNMENTS

> What reform often looks like if it's not system reform is a series of interventions or programs that don't interconnect. The basis of system reform is accepting that education is a complex series of interrelationships and that just changing one aspect has limited scope for change.
>
> (Adrian Piccoli)

The politics of education reform has been largely neglected by academic researchers and this has "left a gap in the knowledge base that reformers need for the design of more effective strategies" (Bruns et al., 2019, p. 36). However, before commencing the case study of how one politician developed one large-scale education system reform, we firstly need to understand the historical context of large-scale system reform and the political and system contexts of politicians as policy makers. This chapter explores those issues and provides the conceptual and theoretical underpinnings for the analysis of case study and the foundations on which new insights and new learnings can be developed.

Three issues for governments in whole system improvement

Since the 1980s, large-scale education system reform has been a major preoccupation of many governments around the world as many developed nations realised their education systems would not be able to lead the way in dealing with the economic, technological and social transformations that were developing globally (Sahlberg, 2016). Government interest, investment and involvement in whole system educational change have continued to increase; however, at the same time, three major issues are converging to create significant problems for governments in improving whole school systems.

Whole system improvement continues to remain elusive

The first problem is that while we have been undertaking large-scale system reform for more than 60 years, we have known for the past 30 years that it is not always delivering the desired system improvement outcomes, despite the enormous investment by governments all over the world and a great deal of research (Fullan, 2016b).

During the 1990s, the development of technology and the internet meant that governments were more easily able to compare their reform efforts and results with what was happening in other countries and lessons about large-scale education reforms became widely available. At the same time, policy makers were becoming frustrated with the frequent failure of the existing approaches to scaling up measured success from one school to many schools (Hopkins et al., 2014). There was also a general dissatisfaction with the seemingly meagre effects of past reform efforts which were not flowing deeply into classrooms and therefore not producing the anticipated improvements in student learning (Supovitz & Taylor, 2005). School improvement activities were leading to disappointing results and questions were emerging as to whether large-scale system reform was actually possible (e.g., Hargreaves & Fullan, 1998; Louis-Seashore, 1998; Sarason, 1990). Research studies in many countries attested to the failure of reform efforts, with neither government policies nor in-school initiatives delivering the widespread or sustainable change that had been expected (Earl et al., 2003; Rolheiser et al., 2002; Teddlie & Reynolds, 2000).

Over the past two decades, it has become even more apparent that reforms are not always achieving the desired outcomes. Student performance is declining in a number of countries (Sahlberg, 2016) and PISA data showed that almost one in every five 15-year-old students performed below the baseline proficiency level on the mathematics assessment (OECD, 2014).

Sahlberg (2004, 2006) captured the growing concerns regarding the failure of reforms to improve student outcomes when he memorably called the prevailing neoliberal orthodoxy in education policy the "Global Education Reform Movement" or GERM, with all its attendant connotations of an uncontrollably spreading virus (Fuller & Stevenson, 2019). Sahlberg (2006, 2016) explored the problematic implications of the GERM and its impact on schooling and identified its features as increased standardisation, narrowing the curriculum to focus on core subjects, the growth of high-stakes accountability and the use of corporate management practices. Edge also noted the "relentless...adoption of increasingly higher-stakes accountability strategies" (2015, p. 203).

Similarly, Hargreaves and Shirley (2009, 2012) called for a move away from what they called the "Three Old Ways" of Innovation and Inconsistency, Markets and Standardisation, and Performance and Partnerships, to the "Fourth Way of Innovation, Inspiration and Sustainability". Harris and Jones (2017) broadened the focus to a society-wide perspective and cautioned that the failure to address the "inconvenient truths" of the big societal system issues of corporatised education, context and culture, inequality and, in some systems, politics and corruption, was limiting or undermining the ability of reforms to deliver change that actually led to improvements.

In their extensive review of the research on the effects of reform efforts at the school and system level, Hopkins et al. (2014) concluded that while much has been learned about how to improve individual schools, and there have recently been ambitious efforts to reform whole systems at district, state and national levels, successful efforts at systemic improvement have been less common. Educational systems continue to demonstrate considerable robustness and resilience in the face of change and whole system improvement – where the vast majority of schools improve – continues to remain elusive (Fullan, 2016b; Fullan & Gallagher, 2020).

No conceptual framework for undertaking large-scale system reform

The second issue which confronts governments is that there is no generally agreed framework for undertaking systems reform.

The increasing frustration with the failure to achieve systemic school improvement led to governments playing an ever more active and central role in externally-developed whole school reform policies and system-level changes, especially in England, the United States, Finland and Canada. At the heart of this increasing focus on systems was the perceived importance of international comparisons and learning from international experience (Campbell, 2015, 2017; Hopkins et al., 2014). This led to considerable research on educational strategies, policies, reform initiatives and outcomes in a large number of countries, as well as a range of international reports and studies which increasingly focused on examining case studies of both schools and reforms across entire national and state education systems[1].

A great deal of this system-level research focused on identifying the factors or elements that contribute to quality system reform. The widely cited McKinsey report, *How the World's Best Performing Systems Came Out on Top* (Barber & Mourshed, 2007), identifies four key factors which focus on high-quality, instructionally-oriented leaders and data-based monitoring of outcomes. However, Levin and Fullan (2008) set out seven different key criteria which focus on goals, motivation, leadership, capacity-building, strategies, resources and communication, while Earl et al. (2003) conclude that the evidence confirms the importance of central policy, school capacity and a strong intervening infrastructure.

The OECD (2015) undertook a comprehensive analysis of international research reports on the factors that contribute to quality education and educational improvement which helpfully drew together the previous research findings. It found that, while each report provided its own specific focus, many researchers agreed that the important policy areas to focus on are teaching and teachers, setting high standards, using data, building capacity, leadership, disadvantaged schools and sound policy making.

More recently, the OECD (2020) has put forward a framework which proposes that for effective policy implementation, the strategy for the policy development process must include three elements. The first is designing a "smart policy" that has a vision, includes appropriate policy tools, such as evidence and system levers, and has the resources available to implement it. The second is "inclusive stakeholder engagement" in the process from an early stage, comprising transparency, involvement and communication. And the third is a "conducive environment" which includes institutions, capacity and policy coherence. Together, these underpin a coherent implementation strategy. However, its focus is on policy implementation and it does not provide a framework for the "smart policy" development stage and nor does it specifically include the role of governments in the process.

While the findings of these studies are not inconsistent, and the OECD (2015) claims that research has increased understanding of school reform and led to a general consensus around what works, what stands out is that the research does not identify any generally agreed set of policies, principles or conceptual or analytical frameworks upon which politicians might draw in developing large-scale system reforms. This is necessary because "Absent such frameworks, practitioners, policymakers and researchers are simply talking past one another" (Spillane, 2013, p. 39).

The stakes are rising

The third, and possibly the most difficult issue for governments, is that the stakes of education reform are rising. Across the Western world, policy makers are convinced that a country's competitiveness in the global economy crucially depends on its ability to develop a knowledge-based economy. Education is seen as a key strategic tool in this process and educational success is viewed as a proxy for economic competitiveness (Earl et al., 2003; Janmaat et al., 2013; Mundy et al., 2016).

The rising use and profile of international student assessments, especially PISA, has increasingly influenced national education policies in a number of countries, and the international comparison of the performance of education systems has become a matter for media headlines (Ball et al., 2012; Breakspear, 2012). This means that governments have no alternative to continuing their involvement in large-scale system reform. While education change may be grounded in a fundamental sense of moral purpose (Campbell, 2017; Fullan, 2010; Hargreaves, 2007, 2020), a lower-than-desired PISA result can affect a nation's reputation and standing internationally, not just in education but economically, and raises inconvenient domestic questions about the competence of governments.

However, while the indicators and metrics of PISA have increasingly been equated with the end goals of education and become "the lens through which we come to understand our systems" (Breakspear, 2014, p. 6), they only measure a narrow range of cognitive skills against a particular conceptualisation of learning outcomes. Breakspear argues that they are "simply too narrow to represent the broader range of goals that school systems are tasked with developing across economic, social, civic and human development domains" (2014, p. 12) and cautions that PISA therefore has potential negative consequences on the policy making processes.

The risk for governments is that politics may drive education policy development to be re-framed around economic ends, while wider educational purposes, which consider what matters in education and what an educated person should be, may therefore be diminished or ignored. Breakspear suggests that no reform should be based on such a single assessment measure and PISA should be used as a starting point for policy insights rather than as a tool for policy action. However, this does not provide politicians with a way to deal with the negative consequences of falling student performance evidenced by such data.

The convergence of these three issues, and the lack of any definitive way forward, confirms the view of Campbell (2017) that there still exists considerable debate and critique about the purposes, approaches and outcomes of policy approaches to transforming education systems within and across countries. The differing views about what makes reforms work, and also why they fail, mean that the applicability and generalisability of the research from one context to another remains problematic (Hopkins et al., 2014). This means there is little clear guidance for politicians, as policy makers, in conceptualising, developing and initiating large-scale education system reform.

What the research does highlight is that many of the factors identified as features of quality reform are contextual, systemic and societal issues which are clearly the province of politicians. Harris and Jones provide a sobering summary of the position:

> The challenges of securing educational change and transformation, at scale, remain considerable. While sustained progress has been made in some education systems generally, it remains the case that the pathway to large-scale, system improvement is far from easy or straightforward… leaving it questionable how far the scholarship of educational change has significantly informed the policy choices that affect schools and school systems.
>
> *(2017, p. 632)*

The problem for politicians is that there are no firm right answers and they are therefore faced with a series of dilemmas and decisions as they design and implement large-scale education system reform (Earl et al., 2003). Indeed, there are indications that their difficulties may be increasing, with Fullan and Gallagher recently claiming that: "More and more people, *including politicians* are becoming convinced that the policy drivers that they have favoured for the past two decades ... do not bring about system change...[and] are actually propelling us backwards" (2020, p. 21, my emphasis).

The role of politicians in policy development

If we are to create guidance for politicians who seek to develop large-scale education system reform, it is firstly necessary to understand not only their role in policy making but also the wider education system and political task environment within which they undertake that role.

Contemporary policy scholars agree that government is at the centre of public policy making and that all policy making is geared towards the single purpose of achieving governmental objectives, whatever they may be (Birkland, 2016; Virani, 2019). As creating new policy instruments and the alignment of policies and programs within a system is at the heart of the theory of systemic reform (Cohen, 1995; Earl et al., 2003), we need to understand the role of politicians in public policy making if we are to gain insights into how they conceptualise, develop and initiate large-scale education system reform.

The role of governments and ministers in public policy making

There is general consensus that passing legislation and setting rules are key roles of government and important system levers in education reform (Angus, 2005; Earl et al., 2003; Whitty et al., 1998); however, there is less agreement on other aspects of the role of governments in education policy. For example, Caldwell (1997) limits it to an overarching one of establishing the framework, setting standards, providing infrastructure and other resources, supporting schools and monitoring outcomes. However, Earl et al. (2003) regard it as a more active one of providing policy coherence while also keeping policy "fresh", maintaining and balancing "high pressure and high support", encouraging local adaptations and innovations, and ensuring ongoing, long-term financial support. I would argue that the roles of governments in education policy will differ and that any of these roles may be appropriate, depending on the specific context.

Given the lack of consensus on the definition of public policy and the role of governments in it, it is not unexpected that there are also differing views as to what is, and what should be, the role of ministers in public policy making.

Some researchers and writers either do not consider the role of ministers at all, or view it as being peripheral; instead, they focus particularly on the role of public servants. For example, while Birkland (2016) describes institutional actors, groups, power and agenda setting as important elements of the public policy process, he does not explore the role of ministers. Wu et al. (2015) create a conceptual framework for "policy capacity" which includes political capacity but puzzlingly omits ministers, even though they claim it "covers all policy processes" (p. 167). Similarly, Moyson et al. (2017) do not mention ministers in their concept of "policy actors", while Hartley et al.'s (2019) characteristics of policy practitioners are specifically for "the twenty-first century public servant". Mukherjee and Bali (2019) use Wu et al.'s (2015) model to consider what constitutes effective policy design in the context of the study and practice of policy formulation, without mentioning the politicians' role apart from "support for the agency" (p. 105).

However, other researchers explicitly recognise the role of politicians in policy making and how it differs from that of public servants. Ball (1994a) sets out five contexts of the policy process: policy influences, policy text production, policy practices/effects, policy outcomes and *political strategies* (my emphasis), while Luetjens et al. (2019) demonstrate the importance of the relationships between the political and public service systems and the need for strong political will and authority for change. Unsurprisingly, researchers who have been senior public servants and have worked closely with ministers, as well as ministers themselves, most clearly support the view that: "A minister (or group of ministers) is pivotal in the policy process" (Edwards, 2021, p. 171).

These studies provide theoretical conceptualisations of the role of governments and ministers in public policy making and also demonstrate that, in many instances, ministers do play a role in the process. However, they do not agree as to what that role might be and nor do they give detailed insights into how politicians themselves conceptualise and operationalise their role in developing policy for whole system reform. As well, the way in which these studies tend to portray ministers as being separate to and different from policy makers highlights how "policy" has often come to mean something quite different from "politics". However, this neglects the reality that often it is difficult to distinguish between them, as every political action has some kind of policy consequence and every policy emerges from some political process (Mitchell & Romero, 2018).

The distinction is also problematic for politicians who may be considering what their role in system reform should be: they are less likely to take a strong leadership role (which may enable them to take a broader and bolder political perspective) if they believe policy making is solely the province of public servants and they are only the passive customers of policy advice. In turn, this may impact on the scope and scale of the reforms which are developed.

The political context of education reform

In the previous section, I explored how the scope of the government's role in public policy making has been theorised, but in practice, the political context significantly influences how politicians develop large-scale education system reforms. This aspect is generally not considered in the field of education policy; however, it is an important part of studies in the politics of education, which is the focus of this section.

As all public policy making is geared towards achieving governmental objectives, its design is embedded in a political task environment. The evidence for this is that sooner or later, the intellectual debate about policy is cut off by political decisions in which politicians take responsibility for the choice of a particular problem definition and its solutions (Hoppe, 2018). For ministers, the challenge of improving education quality therefore faces significant political complexities as major education reform is almost always a highly charged and politicised process (Edwards, 2021; Edwards et al. 2001) where what gets implemented – and its impact – depends as much or more on the politics of the reform process as on the technical design of the reform (Bruns & Schneider, 2016).

However, despite its importance, there is general consensus that very little systematic research actually exists on the politics of reform[2]. Bruns & Schneider contend that: "The core puzzle in education politics is that successful quality reform is so rare despite the large and manifest benefits to individuals, families, and society as a whole" (2016, p. 7). They surveyed "the small academic literature on the politics of reform" and found that education specialists show little interest in politics, concluding that "the politics of education are under-researched and under-analysed" (p. 2). Similarly, in a special edition of the journal *Educational Review* (Fuller & Stevenson, 2019) which focused on deepening our understanding of how the Global Education Reform Movement has developed and been experienced in different jurisdictions, none of the articles considered the role of governments and politicians.

Seemingly in contrast to these studies, Mitchell and Romero's (2018) review of 174 landmark books and articles, in which political scholars have pursued explanations of educational system development, stabilisation and change, contains over 70 titles that include the words "politics" or "political". However, further analysis reveals that only one of them (Zeigler & Johnson, 1972) "uniquely focuses on policymaking processes rather than policy content" (Mitchell & Romero, 2018, n.p.) and none of them focuses specifically on how politics shapes the way in which policy is made by politicians.

Moe claims that political scientists have failed to shed much light on education politics or its far-reaching consequences because "they have not embraced education as a target of comprehensive, in-depth study" (2012, p. 846). Moe and Wiborg contend that:

> The problem lies with the literature itself, and with the fact that, at least for now, there really isn't a there there. No substantive focus. No theoretical coherence. Little or no connection between the various strands of research.
>
> *(2017, p. 10)*

These issues were explored by Bruns and Schneider (2016) in their comparative study of major education reforms which focused on political process issues that arose in the complex and contentious politics of quality reforms. They identified a number of key political decisions that are required in the design of systemic education reform and suggest a short list of recommendations for would-be reformers:

> Consult with leaders of similar reform efforts; identify all actual and potential stakeholders and analyse their interests; assess political capital; assess technical capital; pass core reforms through legislation; divide opponents; make available compensation or side payments; mobilize sympathizers; engage in the battle for public opinion; communicate directly with teachers. (p. 2)

Their research provides valuable insights into the way in which the political context impacts on the design and development of large-scale education system reforms and highlights that this needs to be taken into account in education policy development. It also suggests a potential framework which politicians undertaking such reform may be able to use and provides a checklist intended as a practical tool for reformers. However, they view it as a small beginning, saying:

> The first and most definitive conclusion of this survey is that academic researchers have neglected the politics of education reform and left a yawning gap in the knowledge base that reformers need for the design of more effective policies.
> *(Bruns & Schneider, 2016, p. 53)*

There is agreement that further research is required on the historical and political foundations of education reforms, the role of actors, politics and what parts of the political processes of reform went well or poorly, as these are "still largely a 'black box'" (Busemeyer & Trampusch, 2011, p. 432). While the scope of what might be inside that box is considerable, it is clear that one area for further research is to gain a deeper understanding of how ministers conceptualise large-scale education system reform and undertake the public policy making process of developing it, in the political contexts within which they operate.

What is the system in large-scale system reform?

Before turning to consider this issue in more detail, it is helpful to have a theoretical concept of the education system itself. This will enable us to locate the policy making system and, more specifically, politicians, within the broader education system and consider how they relate to and interact with other parts of it.

During the 1970s and 1980s, education reform began to be characterised by more holistic and systemic approaches, although it did not represent a systematic and coherent approach to school change (Hopkins & Reynolds, 2001; Smith et al., 1992). However, since the 1990s, the focus has increasingly been on systemic educational reform, based on the concept that systemic change is the process of changing a system from one paradigm to another by the application of systems thinking and systems theory (Watson et al., 2008). This was underpinned by the development of complex systems theory which viewed problems and their solutions from the perspective of the whole system (Hoy & Miskel, 2012).

It led to the emphasis on the entire "educational system" as the unit of change, blending program, policy and environmental characteristics and seeking to cohere and align components across a system. This systemic view of education reform is premised on the theory that a coherent complement of programs and policies can produce powerful reform by creating reinforcing and synergistic effects (Cohen, 1995; Smith & O'Day, 1990; Supovitz & Taylor, 2005). This contrasts with individual programs that have limited efficacy because they inevitably run up against constraining and competing efforts and philosophies.

The increasing focus on the "education system" and the idea of "systemic reform" raised the proposition that we can only learn about system change by studying the broader systems in which schools reside and the interactions between them, and working on how to improve them (Datnow et al., 2005; Finnigan et al., 2013). In turn, this led to a rethinking of the conventional narrow definition of an education system as the system of public and private schools that offer students formal education from kindergarten to college graduation, to viewing whole education systems as comprising the local school and community level, the district level and the state or national level, including governments and other agencies (Barber & Fullan, 2005). Hopkins et al. (2014, p. 270) define an educational system as "the entirety of the educational support network for schools" which may include "national systems, state or local systems, or cross school and cross state systems of reform teams".

These definitions remain closely tied to the concept of schools; however, other researchers see the system as extending more broadly. Finnigan and Daly (2014) caution that, while complex systems theory is helpful in understanding the *entire* system of education (their emphasis), it is also important to look beyond the more traditional governmental layers involved in K-12 education, such as local and state educational agencies and the federal government, and extending to what were seen as "outsider" groups, from higher education to foundations, think tanks, advocacy groups and municipal governments.

This more expansive definition of what was included in the "education system" challenged the paradigm of "insiders" and "outsiders" to it. This viewed those who were within schools (teachers and principals, but also school district superintendents) as "insiders", while governments, politicians and other related entities were seen as "outsiders" (Fullan, 1991). While this concept had some theoretical appeal, the distinction between the two proved difficult to maintain in practice, as who was included or excluded by the term "insider" varied from project to project and could also vary from stage to stage within a project (Miller, 2002). It largely fell out of use in the context of complex systems theory and the broadening of the definition of the education system. For example,

Fullan (2016a) changed his language to refer to "external factors" (government and other agencies) to the local school setting (district, community, principal, teacher) rather than "outsiders".

However, more recently, Bruns et al. have undertaken further research which "sought to be extensive in covering the full range of protagonists identified in reform cases across the world" (2019, p. 28) and have returned to the "insider/outsider" paradigm. They identify insider stakeholders as teacher unions, teachers, principals, private schools, education bureaucrats, teacher training institutes, university faculties of education, and government reformers and policy networks. Outsider stakeholders are identified as business, organised civil society and non-government organisations, parents, international development agencies, religious authorities, politicians and political parties. They believe this extended list could have value for reform teams that enter government with little prior experience in government and politics, or in education.

While these lists present a useful starting point, it is likely that they will vary depending on both the jurisdiction and the scope of the reform. For example, in NSW the Education Minister would be considered an "insider" as they have legal responsibilities for various aspects of the system, while "international development agencies" are not a factor.

Ultimately, while these broad parameters are useful in framing our consideration of the education system, in each unique case Lemke and Sabelli's definition is the most relevant and is the one that I am using in this book. They propose that:

> The system must ultimately be defined by our analysis of its constituent elements and environmental dynamics, such as which institutions and social practices and which sources and users of information and material and human resources are tightly enough coupled and interdependent in their behaviour that they must be included within the system.
>
> *(2008, p. 120)*

Locating governments, ministers and policy in the system

These expanded definitions of the education system all include governments, ministers and policy makers; however, where they are located within the system, and how they connect to other elements of it, is less clear.

Initially, open systems theory was essentially a rational planning framework which viewed the education system as a classical formal bureaucratic hierarchy which was tightly managed from the top and internally coherent, like a manufacturing organisation (Cohen et al., 2017). This placed the Minister at the top of the education system pyramid and schools at the bottom.

This was based on the assumption that there was a tight coupling between education policy and what happens in schools and that there was a linear trajectory of change from the top to the bottom of the system (Goldspink, 2007). However, as education systems came to be viewed as complex systems it led to a move away, at least at the theoretical level, from the hierarchical model of educational administration to a more complex, loosely coupled view of the education system. This generally depicts a variety of both insider and outsider stakeholders in a loosely coupled series of connections which may or may not include politicians. For example, while Goldspink includes an entity labelled the "policy centre" in his diagram of a complex education system (2007, p. 41), it is not clear if this comprises governments, including ministers, as well as government agencies and school districts and systems, which also are not otherwise indicated.

Reliance solely on such a model also fails to recognise that education systems are simultaneously both tightly and loosely coupled (Hoy & Miskel, 2012; Peters & Waterman, 1982). They are tightly coupled in terms of the power and legitimate authority relationships between some parts of the hierarchical system, but they are also loosely coupled in terms of the connections within and between the various elements of the broader, complex interconnected system. The tightness or looseness of the coupling will also depend on other factors, such as how centralised or de-centralised is the system. For example, a highly centralised system where schools have little decision-making authority will be more tightly coupled than one where decision-making is decentralised.

More recently, the value of systems thinking in public policy making has been recognised. Althaus et al. (2021) claim that it can help identify who the different stakeholders are and the different spheres of influence and control of each, as well as how problems are understood and addressed and how people and resources are engaged in such processes. This means that in reforming educational systems, we need to be cognisant of both the formal legitimate power and authority relationships that exist between various elements of the system, as well as the formal and informal connections and interactions between them.

The theoretical view which I am taking locates governments and politicians simultaneously at the top of hierarchies, where they exercise legitimate authority in large-scale system reform, as well as in the policy centre as part of a web of interconnected elements, which may be coupled loosely or tightly and where this may vary depending on the context.

The role of Ministers in developing large-scale education system reform

With an appreciation of the role of governments and politicians in public policy making, as well as an understanding of where they are located in the education system, we can now consider the specific role of ministers in developing policy to implement whole system school improvement.

The majority of research in this area has been undertaken by those who were outsiders to the process who, in many cases, did not interview those involved but sourced their information from secondary sources. This means that the voices and perspectives of insiders – the politicians themselves, together with others, such as ministerial office staff, key stakeholders and public servants – are almost entirely absent (Tiernan & Weller, 2010). While outsiders may give us an historical perspective and various interpretations of what occurred and often reveal details that ministers may prefer remain unknown, they cannot know some of the information which would be helpful in giving other insights, particularly into the reasons why ministers behaved as they did. This was recognised by West (1991) in his detailed review of the significant changes to education policy in NSW from 1988 to 1991 which were driven by Premier Nick Greiner and his controversial Education Minister Terry Metherell, when he noted that: "We can never be certain of other people's motives, and it is idle to speculate about them" (p. 57).

Some researchers have attempted to address the lack of insider accounts by interviewing ministers and their staff and quoting their anonymised responses verbatim. For example, Tiernan and Weller (2010) capture the voices of a number of Australian Government ministers, chiefs of staff, ministerial office staffers and senior public servants who were involved in the political process from 2007 to 2009. They provide first-hand insights into how ministers and their offices deal with their departments during the development of policies and the "policy dance" (Bridgman & Davis, 2000) that occurs. However, in relation to large-scale education system reform, there are few insider descriptions by ministers and they are perceived to be of varying quality and usefulness.

In the United Kingdom, Kenneth Baker[3] (1993, 2015) describes what he learnt as an education reformer, including how to change the performance of traditional schools through competition and creating parents as allies against the teacher unions by the publication of school results. Andrew Adonis[4] (2012) has also written about his experiences and what he learned as a reforming Education Minister, positing what he describes as 12 fundamental rules for reformers, couched in simple, direct language. This has been described as "very useful for anyone who wish [sic] to improve the education system in his own country and to build a better society" (Magni, 2013, p. 148). Less helpfully, the memoirs of the discredited and twice-sacked David Blunkett[5] (2006) have been scathingly reviewed as being "a bit of a wet Blunkett" (Hattersley, 2006, p. 23) and described as delusional and self-pitying (Norman, 2006, p. 45).

Most usefully, Leighton Andrews'[6] memoir of transforming the Welsh education sector (2014) describes the challenges of being a minister, including the political context, the policy detail and the ability to communicate with stakeholders and the public. In the book's Foreword, Sir Michael Barber says: "I believe it will be of interest around the world because it enables the reader to see education reform from a minister's perspective, as very few books have done before" (Andrews, 2014, n.p.). He has since been researching and publishing in this specific area (2017, 2018) and his insights as an insider, practitioner and researcher give a balanced perspective to his work.

In Australia, Don Hayward[7] (Caldwell & Hayward, 1998) provides a direct and personal account of the Victorian *Schools of the Future* reforms, including a reflection on the role of the minister. Julia Gillard[8] led major education system reforms to both school accountability for results and school funding[9], and in her memoir (2014), she describes some of the ways in which the design of the reform agenda took into account the political context. These include negotiation with unions; "bundling" popular reforms with ones which were less popular; investing substantial time in outreach to both news media and the business community and having explicit strategies for both; the use of an expert panel on funding reform which drew in key stakeholders and provided both political cover as well as solid technical ideas; and spending substantial time visiting schools across Australia to hear directly from teachers. More recently, Adrian Piccoli[10] has given an insider's account of the power dynamics in Australian education and how the application of that power influences education policy making (Carter & Piccoli, 2024).

These insider perspectives provide a deeper understanding of the role of ministers in the development of large-scale education system reform. However, they are a small sample and it is likely that their views may have been affected by their own investment in the reforms they are describing, so any learnings about the policy making process from them need to be interpreted with caution.

One further area through which the political context of large-scale system reform may be studied relates to the role of the minister's office staff in reform design and policy development. Despite political staff now being institutionalised into the policy process, their role is not well-understood and, according to Taflaga and Kerby (2020), there are calls for increased theorisation around them. Their role is important in reform design as they are located at the intersection of political functions and policy work and, in recent years, political advisers have been recognised as distinct policy actors in their own right (Craft, 2015, 2016; Maley, 2015; Taflaga & Kerby, 2020). However, there are very few insider accounts as to what they actually do or contribute to the process of policy making.

Tiernan and Weller (2010), while not insiders themselves, quote directly from a number of interviews with chiefs of staff and ministerial advisers in their chapter on "Ministers and their private offices". They consider that one of the roles of ministerial staff is "steering policy" and providing a major alternative source of policy advice which includes "helping ministers to engage departments in policy by supervising, orienting and mobilising the work of the department" (p. 262). This is similar to Hollway (1996) who, as an insider, has described the relationship between ministerial offices and departments as an essential partnership that includes policy advising through "close and creative engagement with the Department to analyse issues and identify options, helping the Department to understand the minister's priorities, commissioning policy advice, and providing an overlay to that advice" (personal communication, 2011)[11].

One area where research is missing is any detailed study of the process of the development of a single large-scale education system reform policy in the political context of an Education Minister's office, from the insider perspectives of the minister and his/her staff and also of other insiders to the process such as senior public servants and key education stakeholders. For example, while Luetjens et al. commissioned 20 case studies of successful large-scale reforms in Australia and New Zealand (including such high-profile issues as the response to HIV/AIDS) which describe the role of political leaders and "the importance of the reinforcing interrelationships between the political, policy advisory and implementation systems" (2019, p. xviii), none of the cases focuses solely on the development of the reform from the perspectives of those who were insiders to the process. Such research is likely to be of value in broadening and deepening our knowledge of this aspect of large-scale system reform and is the focus of this book.

With these historical, political and system contexts in mind, we can now turn to a detailed case study of a politician's role in developing one large-scale education system reform.

Notes

1. See Barber and Mourshed (2007), Fullan (2010), Hargreaves and Shirley (2012), Levin (2008), OECD (2015) and Sahlberg (2012).
2. See Gift and Wibbels (2014), Levin (2007, 2010), Moe (2012) and Shrestha et al. (2019).
3. Baker was UK Secretary of State for Education 1986–1989 under Prime Minister Margaret Thatcher.
4. Adonis was UK Secretary of State for Education 2005–2008 under Prime Minister Tony Blair.
5. Blunkett was UK Secretary of State for Education from 1997 to 2001.
6. Andrews was Minister for Education in the Welsh Assembly Government from 2009 to 2013 and is a Professor of Practice at Cardiff Business School.
7. Hayward was Minister for Education in the State of Victoria from 1992 to 1996.
8. Gillard was the Australian Federal Government Minister for Education from 2007 to 2010 and Prime Minister of Australia from 2010 to 2013.
9. Most notably the "MySchool" website and the "Gonski" Funding reforms.
10. Piccoli was Minister for Education in NSW from 2011 to 2016 and was the founding Director of the Gonski Institute for Education at the University of New South Wales.
11. Sandy Hollway, AO, was Chief of Staff to Australian Prime Minister Bob Hawke and later was Secretary of the Federal Department of Employment, Education, Training and Youth Affairs.

PART II
Politics, power and ideology
The development of *Local Schools, Local Decisions*

PART II

3
STARTING THE REFORM PROCESS
Conceptualising the LSLD reform

> Together with the support of some key people we set our broad strategic agenda in opposition and then set about putting it in place, ready for government from day one.
> (Adrian Piccoli)

A key question which arises in the development of large-scale education system reform is: how do politicians conceptualise the reform commitments which they take to an election as "promises", and then implement as policy if they are successful in winning government? It is an important part of the policy development process and can impact significantly on the content of the reform and of the support for it, yet it is one area where research appears to be completely lacking. This chapter provides insights into this part of the process by exploring the initial development of the *Local Schools, Local Decisions* (LSLD) reform while Adrian Piccoli was the Opposition Education Spokesperson[1].

The historical and political education reform context

Policy development is always embedded in its historical and political context, so to understand why and how LSLD was developed, it is first necessary to step back and situate the process within the context of the Australian and New South Wales (NSW) Governments' education policy reforms more generally.

The Commonwealth of Australia is a federal parliamentary democracy under a constitutional monarchy and has three levels of elected governments: the Australian Government; six States and two Territories, each with its own government and parliament; and local government. The State of NSW is located in the south-east of Australia, with Sydney as its capital. It has about one-third of the national population and covers an area larger than Texas, United States. The NSW Department of Education is one of the largest education systems in the world. It is responsible for all government primary and secondary schools (often called public schools) with over 800,000 children (70% of NSW children) attending approximately 2,200 schools. The other two main school education providers are Catholic Education (19%) and the Independent schools sector (11%) (NSW Government, 2021).

Australian education system reform

The Australian Government does not have any direct constitutional powers to make laws regarding education as each of the States and Territories has its own education system and constitutional powers for making policy and laws regarding education. However, it significantly influences education through its powers to make financial grants to the States and Territories and setting requirements relating to policy as a condition of funding.

Its role in Australian schooling was relatively limited and ad hoc until 1973 when Prime Minister Gough Whitlam implemented the radical recommendations of the Karmel Report which included a needs-based funding model to combat inequalities in schooling and a perceived lack of quality in curriculum, pedagogy and school governance (Savage, 2016). This led to the introduction of Australia's first system of recurrent grants from the Australian Government to both government and non-government schools. It was the first national large-scale education system reform and fully systematised the Australian Government's role in education (Lingard, 2000). Since then, its influence in schooling has progressively increased, with reform initiatives in the areas of national curriculum standards, national assessment and reporting, and funding agreements (Savage, 2016). Over the past decades, the States and Territories have also introduced major reforms to their school systems.

NSW education system reform before 2011

In NSW, the history of education policy making has been slow and cautious (West, 1991). It has been hampered by its being one of the largest and most centralised government education systems in the world (Caldwell, 2007; Hingston, 2018) and by a history of conflict between the powerful teachers' union, the NSW Teachers Federation (NSWTF) and both Liberal and Labor governments. From 1988 to 1991, Liberal Premier Nick Greiner and his controversial and abrasive Education Minister Terry Metherell implemented significant changes to education policy, driven by economic rationalism and drawing on the reforms made by the UK Secretary of State for Education, Kenneth Baker, from 1986 to 1989 under Prime Minister Margaret Thatcher. Both the substance of the changes and the manner in which they were done led to mass protests, and the resulting large swing against the Liberal government at the 1991 NSW State Government election was a major factor in limiting further changes (West, 1991).

A Labor Government was elected in NSW in 1995 and remained in power until 2011. Between 1995 and 2003, Premier Bob Carr drove a program of micro-reform, focusing on "standards" and "testing"; however, many of the traditional supporters of public education became increasingly dissatisfied and critics believed Premier Carr had in fact undermined public education (Sherington & Hughes, 2012). The NSWTF and the Parents' and Citizens' Associations of NSW commissioned an independent review which confirmed their concerns that NSW had one of the lowest per capita funding levels for students of all Australian states and one of the highest teacher to student ratios (Vinson et al., 2002). Even for its staunch defenders, the Carr era had been too centralised in operation and not sufficiently school-focused and flexible in its approach (Sherington & Hughes, 2012). There were three different Education Ministers in the six years 2005–2011 and three Directors-General of the Department of Education who had no background in education. So, with no consistent ministerial direction, a focus on cost-cutting, and with financial management overshadowing educational expertise in the administration of public education, few further reform attempts were made, to such an extent that education hardly figured in NSW Labor's 2011 election campaign.

It was not until March 2011, when a new Liberal/Nationals (Conservative) Government was elected and Adrian Piccoli was appointed as Minister for Education, that further large-scale system reforms were introduced in NSW.

Developing a new education reform agenda in NSW

Adrian Piccoli was deputy leader of the National Party, which traditionally represents graziers, farmers and rural voters generally. He had been elected to the NSW Parliament in 1999 at the age of 29, representing a large rural electorate in southwestern NSW, over 100,000 square kilometres in area. He held degrees in Economics and Law and lived in the major regional city of Griffith, 600 kilometres from Sydney. He had held several shadow portfolios in the NSW parliamentary opposition, including agriculture and water, and was appointed Shadow Minister for Education in 2009. He immediately began developing education policies for the next NSW government election, which was scheduled for 26 March 2011.

Piccoli was aware that a key political issue in education in NSW was the centralisation of the government school system and that various reforms regarding the devolution of authority, school autonomy and principal accountability were then in progress between the Australian and State Governments. NSW was already participating in the Australian Government's 2008 *Smarter Schools National Partnership on Improving Teacher Quality* through the *47 Schools Pilot* which increased the recruitment, staffing and funding control in selected schools, and was due to conclude in 2010, before the election. NSW had also committed to the *Empowering Local Schools* reform which proposed financial incentives for 1,000 participating schools (229 in NSW) to "transition to a more independent model", with support for principals on "leading and managing a more autonomous local school" (Gillard, 2010) but which had not yet commenced, pending the conclusion and evaluation of the *47 Schools Pilot*.

These reforms were hot topics of debate in the education world in Australia and in NSW, and the key education stakeholders had differing views about them. Maurie Mulheron, a former President of the NSWTF, told me that the Federation opposed the *47 Schools Pilot*, which they saw as "a bullshit project". However Educational Leader Chris Cane (a pseudonym) said that: "The Public Schools Principals' Forum was pushing hard for greater autonomy for principals, but not so much the Primary Principals' Association and Secondary Principals' Council, and the NSWTF was opposed to it".

In particular, Julia Gillard, then Deputy Prime Minister and Education Minister in the Australian Government (and later Prime Minister) had sparked controversy in 2008 by championing the New York City Schools Chancellor, Joel Klein's neoliberal school reforms of holding principals and teachers to account for the performance of their schools (Beder, 2008). As a Member of Parliament representing a very large rural electorate, Piccoli was appalled by Klein's view that even in a remote area where there was only one school, if it was underperforming, it should be closed, the principal and teachers all sacked and a new school established. He said to me:

> How can you close a school in remote NSW when those teachers are also members of the community and the next closest school may be hundreds of kilometres away? All that does is punish children, families and teachers for the failures of the system.

Engaging with stakeholders

In such a political context, Piccoli believed that consultation would be critical in developing and gaining support for his election policies so he reached out to the key education stakeholders – the NSWTF, the Primary Principals' Association (PPA), the Secondary Principals' Council (SPC) and the Public Schools Principals Forum (PSPF) – and introduced himself to them. He later said of this process:

> No one really trusted us in education, especially not in public education. I set about changing that. Not by what we did. Most of what we did was consistent with our political values of trusting the power of individuals, rewarding effort, being financially responsible and having strong accountabilities in place. I worked very hard to undo the harm that had been previously done and I engaged Primary and Secondary Principals' Associations and the teachers' union from the very beginning.
>
> They actually had a lot to offer. Senior union members visited my electorate whilst I was in opposition and I have had some visit my home to meet my family. Over time we have become quite good friends. But most of all I visited schools, I talked to teachers, I talked to Principals and I listened to what they said they needed.

Through these consultations Piccoli wanted to find out: "Beyond the ideology, what drives them? What is important to them? What are the issues they are facing in their schools?" He said that they told him:

> NSW has historically had one of the most centralised education systems in the world. Everything was very tightly controlled by the centre. Staff were employed and allocated centrally. Almost every funding allocation and the purposes for which it could be used were allocated centrally. Principals often complained that they had very little leadership discretion in the decision making.
>
> The media and politics in general had become obsessed with the results of NAPLAN[2] tests as well as PISA and TIMS results.
>
> Principals made it very clear to me that if they were being held accountable for results, as they increasingly were, then they needed the flexibility to influence those results. Pressure was being applied to teachers, principals and schools to "improve these results". So Principals were right to insist on greater flexibility around who they appoint to their staff and how they allocate the school budget to suit the individual needs of their children. All of these were legitimate concerns that we were determined to do something about.

He also identified that there was a number of growing concerns about the school system itself (Piccoli, 2013):

- Although performing well internationally, Australia was not in the top tier of the high achieving systems – Shanghai, Finland, Hong Kong, Singapore and South Korea.
- The OECD PISA results showed that between 2003 and 2009 Australia as a whole declined in reading literacy.
- NSW had slipped back about half a year against international standards and the proportion of low-performing students was increasing.
- NSW NAPLAN results between 2008 and 2011 showed that there had been little improvement in the results of NSW primary school children, and numeracy results for secondary school students were declining.
- Just under one-third of Aboriginal students across Australia who began high school in 2003 completed the full six years of secondary schooling (about half the rate of non-Aboriginal students from the same year).

During this engagement process, Piccoli made it clear to the stakeholders that he did not support school autonomy (as distinct from the devolution of authority) as an ideological principle that should be applied to all schools, as he believed it would disadvantage rural communities. Instead, his focus was on ensuring that any reforms would empower principals and teachers to decide what was in the best interests of their students and their schools. However, in a speech to the NSWTF Principals' Conference in 2009, he also made it clear that he would place some limitations on the devolution of decision-making to schools, saying that:

> We will not abolish the statewide transfer system[3]. I know some principals want to freely be able to hire who they like, but I come from an electorate with hard to staff schools (and) I cannot support abolishing the system because of the impact it will have on those schools. (Carr, 2009, p. 3)

Conceptualising LSLD

These extensive consultations during 2009 and 2010 formed the basis of the devolution of authority concept for NSW government schools that Piccoli developed as a key election promise by the Liberals and Nationals political parties for the 2011 election. It was called *Local Schools, Local Decisions: Plan to Re-Empower Local School Communities* and was one of 45 promises for *Making NSW Number One Again* through: rebuilding the NSW economy; returning quality services in health, transport, education and community safety; renovating infrastructure; restoring accountability to Government; and returning decision-making powers to local communities (NSW Liberals & Nationals, 2011).

Within this broad framework, the goal of LSLD was to "give more power to principals and school communities to determine how best to meet their individual needs" (NSW Liberals & Nationals, n.d., p. 1). It reflected the issues and concerns which had been identified during Piccoli's consultations and specifically promised to:

- provide $40 million to fund maintenance needs identified by principals and school communities;
- give principals control of the budget for general staff and minor maintenance, and increase it by $20 million;
- allow principals to use local tradespeople and businesses where they offered better value for money;
- undertake an independent public review of the *47 Schools* "Devolution Pilot".

It premised these reforms on a range of detailed, government school specific reasons as to why they were needed. For example, it referenced the Education Department's "Smartbuy" mass procurement policy which required all school supplies (from pens and Band Aids to whitegoods and televisions) to be purchased through the central Procurement Directorate. It claimed that a survey of 500 principals had found that in many cases the Smartbuy prices were 20–40% higher than local retailers, the exemption process was so long it was not possible to take advantage of special offers and the policy disadvantaged local businesses in regional NSW (NSW Liberals & Nationals, n.d., p. 4).

While the LSLD election promise made no reference to any ideological basis for the proposed reforms and did not use the word "autonomy", it was clearly founded on the belief that decisions are best made by the people they affect and as close as possible to the places where they will have an impact. However, it did not appear to connect with other election promises regarding financial control, accountability and reducing unnecessary expenditure. This would later become a political issue, as will be seen in the next chapter.

Insights from stakeholders

Piccoli's extensive consultations, and ensuring that the election commitments addressed the real issues in schools, won favour with the key education stakeholders whom I interviewed.

Liliana Mularczyk (former President of the NSW SPC) said: "Piccoli wanted honesty and open book responses and we valued and respected that. The relationship of openness, trust and respect grew from there".

Jim Cooper (former President of the NSW PPA) said the principals' associations particularly appreciated his understanding of rural schools, as did the NSWTF which said: "He has in the past expressed an understanding for the difficulties faced by rural schools and … repeatedly acknowledged the importance of the transfer system in ensuring statewide teacher recruitment, retention and distribution" (Carr, 2011, p. 5).

Maurie Mulheron (former President of the NSWTF) recalls that senior union members took Piccoli to visit schools and introduce him to principals and that Piccoli "seemed like a breath of fresh air" as he was "not aggressive" and "didn't hang up the phone" on union officials, which was in contrast to their hostile relationship with the Department of Education at that time. The union thought he was listening and felt "a little bit reassured" regarding the devolution agenda, although he seemed "extraordinarily naïve" about the public school system. The NSWTF also commented that: "We have appreciated the positive and professional relationship Mr Piccoli maintained with Federation while in Opposition and we look forward to this continuing now that he is the Minister" (Lipscombe, 2011, p. 16).

These positive comments from a union, which was traditionally politically allied to the Labor Party and opposed to Liberals and Nationals Governments, show that Piccoli's willingness to consult, listen and take action to ensure that the policies he was developing addressed the real issues in schools, especially in rural areas, rather than being wedded to an ideological position or an overarching election promise, had begun to build trust and respect with stakeholders, even before he became Minister. As will be seen, these relationships were also an important factor in the Minister's ability to manage the political issues which arose during the development of the policy.

My own experience as one of these stakeholders provides insights into how Piccoli was not only willing to engage and listen, but also prepared to revise his policy thinking in response. I was the Chief Executive Officer of KU Children's Services, the oldest and one of the largest early childhood education and care not-for-profit providers in Australia. I had never met Piccoli and he had not engaged with the sector because it was in the Labor Government's portfolio of community services (largely a welfare portfolio) at that time, and not in education.

About nine weeks before the 2011 election, I heard that Piccoli was planning to announce a policy that if the Liberals/Nationals won government they would move preschools to the education portfolio and leave all other child care, including long day care, in the community services portfolio. The sector supported moving all Ministerial responsibility for early childhood education and care to education; however, we were strongly opposed to conceptually splitting the sector into "education" and "child care", as this was against all best practice thinking, and it would also have been extremely difficult for providers to be regulated through two separate government departments. So, with the support of my fellow not-for-profit early childhood sector CEOs, I sought a meeting with Piccoli to give him our views.

Piccoli was in his electorate campaigning, so I made the one and a half hour flight to Griffith to meet him. I advised him why the stakeholders thought his plan was bad policy, provided some international evidence and put the case for instead moving all of early childhood education and care to the education portfolio, which would have the strong support of the sector. After about 15 minutes he said: "Yes, I can see what you are saying and I don't think we have thought this through properly. Can you write me a new policy?" I said "yes" so we went for a coffee and discussed a number of education reform issues and I delivered the new policy to him before I caught the afternoon flight back to Sydney. During a campaign speech to the early childhood sector stakeholders a couple of weeks later, he announced a new election policy that all early childhood would be transferred to the education portfolio. This was very well-received by the sector and it was included in his portfolio responsibilities when he was sworn in as Minister.

As a stakeholder, three things impressed me. The first was his willingness to engage with me about a policy issue at such a late stage of the election campaign. The second was his real interest in the evidence I presented to him and in the views of the sector. And the third was his willingness to change his planned policy to one which he believed was better on that basis.

This engagement also had one completely surprising and unanticipated consequence for me personally. Piccoli and I continued to have discussions about public policy and public sector reform during the next two months in the lead up to the election. And the day after he was sworn in, I became his Chief of Staff and resigned from my CEO role.

Analytical Reflection

According to Bruns and Schneider, the politics of education reform are "under-researched and under-analysed" (2016, p. 2). One area where research appears to be completely lacking is how Opposition politicians conceptualise and develop the large-scale system education reform commitments which they propose to take to election and then implement as policy if they are successful in winning government. This aspect of the political process is entirely absent in three recent major comparative studies on the politics of education reform (Bruns & Schneider, 2016; Busemeyer & Trampusch, 2011; Shrestha et al., 2019). The overview of the initial conceptualisation and development of the LSLD reform in this chapter therefore provides a number of new insights into this aspect of reform development.

Firstly, it helps to locate the reform within its complex *historical and political context*. The importance of this has been highlighted by Hargreaves and Goodson who found that most mainstream educational change theory and practice neglects the political, historical and longitudinal aspects of change, arguing that: "Sustainability of educational improvement, in its fullest sense, is unlikely to occur without a theory and a strategy that is more historically and politically informed" (2006, p. 35). The large-scale education reform strategy to devolve authority and give more power to principals was shaped by an *historical context of concern* that 16 years of an increasingly centralised government school system in NSW was not delivering the desired student outcomes and by *a political context* where school autonomy and principal accountability were contentious issues of public debate.

The case assists our understanding of the politics of education reform by showing how the initial conceptualisation and discourse regarding the development of a large-scale system reform policy *occurred through an entirely political process* which was outside the more usual processes of public policy development by Ministers and public officials. It also confirms Pont's view (2018) that education policy making depends on "the 3 Ps" – policy, politics and people – and that education change specialists, policy analysts and policy makers must factor the political and economic contexts and the educational environment into education reform development, as the content cannot be separated from the process.

Secondly, it shows how *engagement and consultation with stakeholders at the very earliest stages of large-scale system reform development* play an important part in shaping the reform. This is consistent with research by Bruns and Schneider (2016) who found that an understanding of stakeholders' likely responses is critical to key decisions on the design of systemic education reform, and that consulting informally early and often with them is the best way to gauge their preferences and anticipate their reactions. It also aligns with Shrestha et al.'s (2019) finding that getting the buy-in of key stakeholders, such as teachers' unions, is vital for introducing and implementing reform.

The case study shows how Piccoli leveraged both the historical and political contexts to gain the support of key stakeholders, who would normally be opposed to any reforms proposed by the conservative parties, by engaging in discourse with them for two years before the release of the LSLD election commitment, which responded to their concerns. The political value of this approach to reform design was demonstrated when the NSWTF did not attack the Liberals and Nationals education election promises during the election campaign, even though they were ideologically opposed to such reform. As will be discussed in the following chapters, it would also prove important in developing the policy in its final form.

The somewhat surprised comments by the educational leaders regarding Piccoli's willingness to engage with stakeholders and listen to them also indicate that failure to consider the place of Opposition politicians in policy making is common, even though its benefits can be considerable, as we can see in this case. Piccoli fully understood this and used it to his advantage, later saying:

> It's a common mistake for those who seek to influence government policy, be they academics, think tanks or unions, not to lobby the "next government" – the Opposition.
>
> I spent two years as the opposition spokesman for education and learned an enormous amount in that time. It was a golden opportunity to influence the next government. I visited lots of schools and I made strong contacts with heads of the government, catholic and independent sectors. I also made strong links with Principal groups as well as public education union representatives. I got to understand the key influencers in education. I learned what we agreed on and what we disagreed on. And I learned what they disagreed with each other about – information that would prove useful in later years. I learned what pressures they were under from their own constituencies.
>
> Together with the support of some key people we set our broad strategic agenda in opposition and then set about putting it in place, ready for government from day one.

Thirdly, this gives rise to an interesting perspective on the complexity of the education system and begs the question: *where are Opposition politicians located conceptually in the system?* As discussed in the previous chapter, the complex education system framework proposed by Goldspink (2007) does not even seem to envisage that they have a place in the system as they cannot be categorised as being in the "policy centre" and nor are they an "interest group". In fact, they are in a unique position of having the soft power of being a Member of Parliament, who, if elected, may become a Minister and gain the legitimate authority and hard power of being able to implement election promises as government policy.

This lack of a clear conceptual understanding of their place in the system may be one reason why stakeholders and opposition politicians do not engage more. However, we have seen in this case study how significant benefits of policy influence can accrue from a relatively small investment of time and resources, so it is suggested that greater focus on this aspect of policy making by all parties could be beneficial.

Finally, this overview of the conceptualisation of LSLD provides an insight into the *processes through which policies are developed.*

There are many possible ways to define public policy, based on different intellectual backgrounds and epistemological assumptions; however, these often ignore or conflict with each other and academic studies have been unable to reach a consensus definition (Birkland, 2016; Peters & Zittoun, 2016). Despite this lack of agreement, Birkland suggests that a consideration of all the variants of the definition enable us to discern its key attributes as being: that government policy is "public"; it is a response to a problem; and it is made by government. At its simplest, a policy can be regarded as a text: "A statement by government of what it intends to do, such as a law, regulation, ruling, decision, order, or a combination of these. The lack of such statements may also be an implicit statement of policy" (Birkland, 2016, p. 9). In NSW, the political and historical context gave rise to a problem which required attention and therefore provided grounds for the development of an election commitment to address it.

However, as Stephen Ball has argued, these kinds of linear, two-dimensional representations do not reflect the complexities and the messy reality inherent in how policy is produced by governments and politicians, and fail to recognise the "discontinuities, compromises, omissions and exceptions" (1990, p. 3). He instead theorises that policy is both text *and* discourse: policy texts are both "products and tools of production" (contested, mediated and differentially represented by different actors in different contexts) (Ball, 1994a, p. 19; 2015, p. 311), whereas policy discourses are "ways of talking about and conceptualizing policy" (produced and formed by taken-for-granted and implicit knowledges and assumptions about the world and ourselves) (Ball, 1994b, p. 109; 2015, p. 311). This is also consistent with the view of Schneider and Ingram that policies are not just contained in laws and regulations but are also "revealed through texts, practices, symbols, and discourses that define and deliver values including goods and services as well as regulations, income, status, and other positively or negatively valued attributes" (1997, p. 2).

The case study exemplifies Ball's theory, as the LSLD election promise evolved through an extensive two-year process of "policy as discourse" between an Opposition politician and the education stakeholders, to "policy as text" in the form of the *Local Schools, Local Decisions: Plan to Re-Empower Local School Communities*. LSLD had become a Liberals and Nationals election promise which, if they were elected to government, would become a government policy that Piccoli would be expected to deliver and against which his performance as a Minister, and his and the new Government's trustworthiness in keeping election promises, would be judged (Pétry, 2014).

The stakes of LSLD were therefore high and, as we will see in the next chapter, the process was only just beginning.

Notes

1 Also known as the "Shadow Minister".
2 NAPLAN is the Australian National Assessment Program in Literacy and Numeracy.
3 This supported schools in regional and rural areas through providing system-wide incentives for teachers to teach in schools in less-desirable locations.

4
ENCOUNTERING AND ALIGNING COMPETING REFORM GOALS

> Ministers play an essential role in policy making by clearly articulating their policy intent to public servants in their departments, teachers, schools, and key education stakeholders.
>
> (Adrian Piccoli)

On Saturday 26 March 2011, the Liberals and Nationals Coalition was elected to form government in NSW, with a large majority. Ministers were sworn in on Sunday, 3 April 2011, and I commenced as Chief of Staff to the new Minister for Education, Adrian Piccoli, on 4 April 2011. We immediately set to work on establishing our Office and beginning the implementation of the promises and reform agenda the Minister had taken to the election. As these had been clearly laid out in the election documents, our expectations were that this would proceed quite smoothly; however, to our surprise, this turned out not to be the case. In fact, five competing policy and political goals for the *Local Schools, Local Decisions* (LSLD) reform unexpectedly became apparent to us during the first four months in government. This not only delayed the development of the policy but also had the potential to reframe LSLD around a managerialist ideology of savings and efficiencies, rather than being focused on the Minister's promise of devolution of decision-making in the interests of schools and students.

Encountering competing reform goals

The Minister's goal

The first goal was that of the Minister himself. He told me that he viewed LSLD as a specific election commitment which he would be accountable for delivering, as well as a way to address the concerns principals had expressed to him. His goal was to give more power to principals, teachers and school communities to decide what was in the best interests of their students and their schools in such areas as staffing, purchasing and infrastructure, within a strong public school system, rather than extensive autonomy. He wanted "to put students at the centre of every decision we make about their education" and "to lift education performance across all schools" (Piccoli, 2014, p. 2).

We did not discuss whether there was any evidence that increased authority improved student outcomes, as it did not seem necessary: empowering local schools was a key tenet of both the major Australian political parties, and as it was an election commitment, our task was to develop the details of the policy and get it implemented. It was both a political and an educational priority and Piccoli wanted to get to work on it straight away.

The Government's goal

The second goal was that of the Government. While this might have been expected to be the same as the Minister's goal, this was not exactly the case.

It was set out in a "Charter Letter" which the new Premier, Barry O'Farrell, handed to each Minister at the first Cabinet meeting of the incoming government on 3 April 2011. These letters officially marked the transition from Opposition to Government by formalising the election commitments into the overall policies of the Government, and by giving specific, personalised directions to each Minister as to what their goals and priorities should be in developing and implementing them, thereby galvanising momentum for the reform to be developed and implemented (Shrestha et al., 2019).

His Letter to Piccoli set out the Key Commitments that "frame the Government's intentions and direction in Education" together with 17 specific "individual policy and program commitments to be delivered" plus a further thirty activities which covered the entire scope of education in NSW and totalled over $323 million in new expenditure. The second of these was to "Implement the *Local Schools Local Decisions* policy": LSLD was therefore just one of a wide range of reforms the Minister would have to quickly begin to address.

The Charter Letter required the Minister to bring to the Expenditure Review Committee of Cabinet (ERC) in June 2011 "all program and policy details, costings, and implementation plans for our election commitments in your portfolio". However, it contained no indication that the Minister would be required to make any Budget savings. The reason for this omission is unclear as it would soon become apparent that savings were indeed an expectation by ERC and this would become a major issue in developing the LSLD reform.

Interestingly, while the Charter Letter had a clear focus on having a world-class and more equitable education system, there was no specific "education goal". This did not appear to be a problem as the Minister's goal was not incompatible with the expectations in the Charter Letter. However, the lack of a clearly specified government goal would become a crucial factor in the development of LSLD, as which goal would prevail became not only a test of competing ideologies, but also of the Minister's ability to wield power to achieve the reform he had promised to stakeholders.

The Better Schools Taskforce goal

To the surprise of both the Minister and myself, we soon discovered that there was a third goal at play in the Department.

Piccoli believed that his "most significant role was to set the strategic direction for the Education Department in line with the broad direction of the government". He knew that a good relationship with the Department would be critical in delivering the reform agenda, so on his election he had acted immediately to begin to build trust with the public servants, as he had done with the education stakeholders while he was in opposition.

Educational Leader Chris Cane (a pseudonym) told me that, although some of the Department executives had met Piccoli, he had no relationships with them, as Opposition Members of Parliament in the Westminster system cannot talk to public servants officially. Two days after the election, before he was even sworn in as Minister, he therefore surprised them when he "turned up at the Department" saying he had "just come to say hello" and had "brought the [incoming] Treasurer" with him. Cane said that this was seen as a "real positive" and "good start" as he had "made the effort to come in and talk".

The Minister and I agreed that our first official priority was to meet the new Acting Director-General of the Department of Education, Ms Pam Christie[1] to ensure she was clear about his goals and priorities. We also needed to find out what policies the Department was already working on, what they were seeking to achieve and how far advanced they were, to provide the starting point for our reform development. He arranged for her to meet us in his Ministerial Office in Parliament House on Monday, 4 April 2011, the day after he was sworn in and my first day as his Chief of Staff. This wide-ranging briefing meeting then continued at different times and in different locations over the following three days, with other Department Executives attending for various matters.

One issue we became aware of was the "Better Schools" reform plan which the Department had been working on for some time and which Chris Cane later described as "the catch-all for all the bright ideas stuck in the bottom drawer". Cane told me that Ms Christie had instructed the Executive Director Financial Services not to present Better Schools at these initial "meet and greets" as she intended to set up a formal briefing for the Minister on it later. However, when the Minister asked about new ideas for reform, the Executive Director "disobeyed and slapped it on the table" and "the Minister's eyes lit up and he was excited at the idea".

Now aware of its existence, the Minister requested a further briefing and on 14 April 2011, he and I were given a presentation by the "Better Services and Value Taskforce". The Executive Director Financial Services told us that the Better Schools reforms were to improve decision-making in and about NSW public schools and were required because there was a "fundamental mismatch between authority, funding and accountability – they don't line up". However, he made no mention that Better Schools was intended to drive efficiencies or to make savings. He advised us that the document was in the final stages of development and offered to provide a full presentation once it was completed, which was expected in June.

At that time, neither the Minister nor I recognised that this briefing was the first indication that the goals of the Taskforce developing Better Schools might not be aligned with the Minister's goal for devolving more authority to schools. On reflection, the name of the Taskforce – "Better Services and Value" – and the fact that neither of its two senior leaders were educators, should probably have flagged to us that there might be a problem. However, the wider political and operational context, as seen in the Charter Letter, impacted our ability to recognise this at that time. We had been in office for only ten days and were preoccupied with many other things, including appointing the first Minister's Office staff and having a range of meetings. (That same day, the Minister and I also had our first meetings with ten key school education stakeholders, the key vocational education and training stakeholder, and then flew to Melbourne to attend his first meeting of the National Ministerial Council on Education.)

However, on reflection, we were too trusting and we did not probe sufficiently. We therefore did not pick up that the advice we were being given was the advice they thought we wanted to hear, rather than what we needed to know.

The Treasury and the Expenditure Review Committee's goal

As a result of our failure to recognise that Better Schools was not aligned with the Minister's goal and expectations, it was only when we attended our first meeting with ERC on 10 May 2011 that it became apparent to us that there was a fourth goal in play and that the issue of competing goals might be a problem.

Perhaps naively, I had assumed that ERC would operate like a public service or business organisation committee, where issues would be raised, options for action put forward and evidence as to their costs and benefits weighed before a decision was made. Instead, the Minister and I quickly discovered that, while such issues were generally detailed in the papers before the Committee, it was also a forum where Treasury officials sought to exert their power and influence over Ministers and Departments. Piccoli said of it:

> The most important sub-committee of Cabinet is the Expenditure Review Committee. Every funding proposal must go through it. The Treasurer chairs it and it has the Premier, Deputy Premier, Minister for Finance and two other senior Ministers on it.
> It is an exercise in power intimidation.
> Not only the Ministers attend but so does the Secretary of their departments, Chiefs of Staff and other people who I never ended up finding out why they were there. Ministers and Secretaries get quizzed on finances, whether budgets are being kept and whether new funding proposals could be funded from anywhere except Treasury. It was a very weird experience.
> This is usually where the battles with the Treasurer and Treasury began.

The discussion at ERC focused on how savings could be achieved in the Education Budget generally and in public schools in particular. The Treasurer said that ERC "is behind the Better Schools Program" and asked: "What services could be cut in Better Schools? Can we be more aggressive on Better Schools reform? How much more can we get out of it?"

The Department Executive Director Financial Services, who was at the meeting, suggested that increasing class sizes in public schools was the only way to meet the savings targets and that the budget would be unachievable if that did not occur. However, Minister Piccoli pushed back, saying that the pressure was to reduce class sizes and it would be politically unacceptable to increase them, and both the Premier and Secretary of the Treasury agreed that class sizes were "off the table". Finally, it became apparent that we would not reach a solution that day and the Treasurer said: "Let's come back and see what we can do".

This focus by the Treasurer on using Better Schools to drive savings in schools came as a surprise to the Minister and me. The Charter Letter required the Minister to deliver new policies costing $323 million, including the commitment of $60 million for LSLD. We had therefore expected that ERC would allocate this additional funding to the Budget, not use the devolution of authority as a means to make budget cuts through the Department's proposed Better Schools Program.

Also, only five days before ERC, the Minister, Ms Christie and I had met with the Premier and the Director-General of his Department to discuss the Charter Letter and how the Premier would assess the Minister's performance. This included his Budget deliverables; yet any expectation of savings in schools was not mentioned, let alone that Better Schools might be used to drive them. Similarly, the Minister and I had met with a senior staffer in the Premier's Office about the State Plan on the same day as ERC. The Minister had described Better Schools as "a proposal for local decision making, principal devolution, and broad-banding funding" and no one raised that it might be used to drive budget cuts.

The ERC meeting made it clear to us that not only did Treasury have a budget savings goal for Better Schools, but that the Department executives were aware of it and had failed to brief us about it at either the Better Schools presentation on 14 April or in preparation for ERC. The Minister therefore demanded an urgent meeting the next day with Ms Christie and the senior Education executives who had been at ERC, at which he expressed his displeasure. He told them that the ERC meeting would have been easier with an understanding of the big picture of "how the savings fit into the whole Budget" and that Better Schools needed a context which he expected them to provide.

Now that we were alerted to the Better Schools and Treasury/ERC savings and efficiencies goals for LSLD, the Minister and I started to address this in the political context. We met with the Treasury Secretary and Deputy Secretary on 25 May 2011 to clarify exactly what they expected from Better Schools. They said they anticipated a report back to ERC on the "overall Department savings plan", whether "other courageous things can be put in place", and "to what extent Better Schools can be a vehicle for driving more flexibility".

This political push by Treasury and the Premier's Office to use Better Schools to drive savings continued during June, and the budget goal of Treasury and ERC became increasingly apparent to us. The Department's Executive Director Financial Services advised me that they had managed to identify efficiencies that would achieve a 1% saving in Better Schools but Treasury was after 1.5%. Similarly, a senior political staffer in the Premier's Office told me that Better Schools needed to drive a review of school-based staff, including reducing school support officers and administrative staff, to make savings.

By the end of June 2011, the Minister had been in office for almost three months but there had been no action on developing the LSLD reform. At the same time, it had become apparent that the Minister, ERC, Treasury and the Better Schools Taskforce had different and competing goals as to what it was expected to achieve. Nor had the Department provided any policy document which identified what and how much authority they were proposing might be delegated to principals, although, according to Chris Cane, Better Schools had been in preparation for two years. Even references to the specific LSLD election promise had dropped off the reform agenda and been replaced by the "Better Schools" language and ideology.

Crucially, no one was taking the lead on resolving the issue. The Minister and his Office were being mainly reactive to the other political players who were pursuing their own agendas. Nor had the Minister given strong and explicit directions to the Department, so they lacked guidance as to his expectations in providing their policy advice. Resolution of these issues, including a clear statement of the desired outcomes for the reform, was urgently required before any coherent policy on the devolution of authority to schools could be developed.

The turning point: the "Better Schools" Presentation

By late June 2011, not only was it apparent that the goals of the Treasury and the Better Schools Taskforce were not aligned with those of the Minister, but we were concerned that the public servants seemed to know much more about exactly what Better Schools was proposing than either the Minister or me.

The first step in our gaining some control of the reform agenda was to ensure we had all the available information, so the Minister requested that the Department provide a full and detailed presentation, together with copies of the Better Schools document. This was held in the Minister's Office on 30 June 2011. In addition to the Minister and our policy staff and Department Liaison Officers[2] involved in LSLD, I invited all our policy and media staff to attend as I already knew from experience that having them review proposed policy documents more broadly often averted potential problems. The Department Executive Directors gave a lengthy PowerPoint presentation and provided several copies of their 245-page proposed consultation document, entitled *Better Schools, Better Services* (BSBS). The Minister read it on the plane home to Griffith that afternoon and rang me the next morning. My notes of what he told me said:

> Consultation Doc is RUBBISH. Better Schools needs to be rewritten – on Agenda for Monday.
> Don't understand what will happen at schools. Doesn't say what it means to schools. Doesn't make sense if you haven't lived it. Driven by what reforms mean to Dept, not to principals, what happens for them. How will it support getting better educational outcomes? Individual schools have individual needs and they need to be able to meet them.
> Be firmer about it. We are going to do these six things: "staffing, broad-banding funding, procurement." We want to consult about the details. Don't consult about the "why", consult about the "what".
> Be bolder. We are going to do this. Consult on the detail. Political context.

At our Minister's Office staff meeting with Minister Piccoli the following Monday (4 July 2011), we analysed the BSBS document. All the senior policy staff and DLOs had read it over the weekend and we discussed what we should do next.

The Minister's major concern was that the "suggestion from the Department for consultation was 'whether devolved decision-making was a good idea or not' ... whereas the consultation we wanted to do was 'what things did principals want control over and how much control did they want?'". He was also worried that "they are putting layers of complexity that aren't necessary onto principals". He told us he believed that it was not appropriate as a consultation document because it "was all management-speak", and he was "bored at page 7".

DLO Kim Kirk (a pseudonym), who was a media and communications expert, also expressed serious reservations regarding the appropriateness of the document as a mechanism for consultation. Kirk drew our attention to a particular diagram which was used several times, saying it seemed to conceptualise schools as being rooted in a dominant Department State Office flower pot, with students and staff depicted only as pale flower petals, having equal status with things such as peers and local governance, rather than being at the heart of the system and the focus of the reforms. Kirk said it was particularly concerning that "teachers" were not specifically included in the diagram at all, which was likely to be extremely offensive to them.

More concerningly from a media and political perspective, Kirk scathingly described this diagram as "Flowerpot Nation", referencing the Australian Labor Party's 2001 education policy entitled "Knowledge Nation", which is mainly remembered for its "incoherent diagram" (Barker, 2006) that was publicly ridiculed by the then Liberal Government as a "spaghetti policy" and referred to as the "Noodle Nation" (Australian Politics, 2001). That had not only doomed it as an election policy but made its title an on-going Australian political by-word for complex and incomprehensible policy documents. Kirk said that the Better Schools proposed consultation document had a similar potential to become a laughing stock politically, which would be humiliating for the Minister and also ensure the failure of LSLD.

This Minister's Office meeting, where we analysed BSBS in terms of both its policy and political implications, was the "critical moment" in the reform development process (Shrestha et al., 2019, p. 9) when the Minister began to proactively exercise his political power to secure control of the reform agenda and to take the lead on the development of LSLD. It brought four critical issues into sharp focus for the first time.

Firstly, the Minister realised that *the Better Schools reform was not about delivering the LSLD election promise of devolving decision-making to schools* (it was not even mentioned in the 245-page BSBS document). It had been developed by senior Department officers who were not educators and had been driven by Treasury pressuring the Department to make efficiency cuts. Its goals were a combination of neo-liberal efficiency-driven, managerialist and administrative measures, clearly directed at meeting budget savings targets, while shifting any blame for loss of function to schools. This was not acceptable to the Minister as it did not meet his own goals for the reform and failed to address the Government's goal set out in the Charter Letter direction to implement the LSLD election promise. It also did not accord with the assurances he had given to the key stakeholders during the consultation process.

Secondly, Better Schools *failed to recognise that the LSLD election policy had already promised that authority would be devolved to schools.* Instead, it was mainly devoted to exploring whether devolved decision-making was a good idea or not, drawing heavily on research findings in the recently released McKinsey report (Mourshed et al., 2010).

Thirdly, the length and *Flowerpot Nation complexity of the document made it inappropriate for use as a consultation document.* It used the style and academic language of a consultant's report and did not engage with the critical policy questions of how much and what types of authority should be devolved, and to whom.

Finally, on the positive side, *it provided valuable evidence which supported devolving authority to schools.* The Minister highlighted one of its conclusions: "There is a strong inverse correlation between a school system's stage on the improvement journey and the extent to which tight central control is exercised over the activities and performance of individual schools". This increased our confidence in the policy direction we were taking on devolution.

This detailed understanding of *BSBS* and its implications convinced us that it was not fit for purpose as a consultation document to inform policy development and it also represented a political risk to the Minister. We realised that we needed to stop being reactive to the demands of Treasury and the reform program ideas of Better Schools, as we had been for the previous three months, and instead to proactively take charge of the process of developing the LSLD reform. The Minister said:

> For me the memorable moment was when we decided not to ask whether schools wanted more authority in the consultation but rather to ask them how much authority do they want. I remember this being about jumping ahead a few steps in the consultation so we didn't waste time getting bogged down in whether authority was a good idea or not.
> We were more ambitious than the Department and we had decided it was.

The Minister was now focused both on taking the lead as a policy maker and on managing the political context to ensure LSLD achieved both his educational policy goals and the Government's political goal of devolution, rather than the ideological and managerial goals of Treasury, ERC and the Better Schools Taskforce.

Aligning the reform goals and defining the outcomes

The Minister and his Office next set about addressing the political and public policy process issues in order to align the disparate reform goals with his own and to clearly define the outcomes that the LSLD reform would be expected to achieve.

For the Minister to regain control of the reform agenda and mandate the change in direction from Better Schools, it was firstly essential to know what the educators within the Department and the education stakeholders in the wider system thought of it, as they had not been included in the Better Schools Taskforce. DLO Mel Marsh (a pseudonym) therefore reached in to the Schools Directorate (from whence they had been seconded) and out to the principals' associations (with which, as a former principal, Marsh already had strong connections) and confirmed that it had no traction. None of the educators supported the language or title of *Better Schools, Better Services* and saw it as "management lingo and service/efficiency driven ... with no education content". This would provide the Minister with a strong support base for combating the Better Schools and Treasury focus on efficiencies and savings.

It also led us to the belated realisation that the Better Schools goal was not the only reform goal in play within the Department. In the Schools Directorate, there was yet another goal: "To give the teachers and principals who work with students every day more authority to adapt what they do and how they do it to meet the needs of their students".

So now there were four goals in all – two focused on the needs of students and schools and two on efficiencies and savings. The knowledge that there were differing views on the devolution policy in two parts of the Department, and that the goals of the educators were aligned with those of the Minister, opened up the opportunity for the Minister's Office to ensure the views of these educators were included in the development of the LSLD policy.

At the same time, the Minister leveraged the strong relationships he had already developed with the three principals' associations and the NSW Teachers Federation by calling them to confirm the discussions he had had with them regarding the LSLD election promise: that if principals were to be held accountable for results, they should have more control of the inputs into their students' performance. The agreement to this by principals' associations showed that there was also a fifth goal in the mix: for principals to be empowered to decide what was in the best interests of their students and their schools and allocate resources accordingly. However, as we expected, the NSWTF was opposed to both the savings and efficiency goals as well as to the devolution of authority to principals. Maurie Mulheron told me they believed that it was an "ideological attack on public education provision" and was not needed, as schools were restricted "due to a lack of budget resources not a lack of authority".

We had now identified that there were five goals in play and we also had the assurance that three of the goals were already aligned (those of the Minister, the education stakeholders and the Schools Directorate of the Department). This led to action by the Minister and his staff on a number of political and policy fronts simultaneously during July 2011.

The key issue was that these conflicting goals had to be dealt with in the political context, where there were many different power and authority relationships in play in a complex open system, rather than a simple system with the Minister at the apex of a system hierarchy.

While the Minister had *legislative power and administrative authority* over the Department and could direct public servants to provide him with policy advice, one of the features of the Westminster system of government is that he *could not direct them as to what that advice should be*. (This situation, where there is no policy yet in existence, is very different from the authority hierarchy that comes into play when there is a policy in place, as the Minister can then direct the public service to implement it.) As well, while the Minister was accountable to the Premier for the delivery of the education election commitments, he *did not have authority over the goals set by the Treasurer and ERC.*

In this complex system, the Minister lacked the authority and formal "hard" power to direct what the policy advice would be. And while he could have simply rejected Better Schools and mandated a devolution policy by Ministerial direction, ERC still held the formal power to impose budgetary savings measures that would have made it unworkable[3]. This meant that before the LSLD policy could be determined, political goal alignment had to be achieved through the Minister's use of "soft" power, of which he said:

> Ministers have power that comes with their office. Normal people call it power – politicians call it political capital. But this is not the real power Ministers need in order to make change. True power is the soft power to influence, the power to cajole, the power to motivate, the power to inspire others to follow.

In exercising this soft power in such a complex system, one of the first things the Minister did was symbolic. The education stakeholders had made it clear that they did not support the Department's reform title of *Better Schools, Better Services* as it came with baggage that would make it unacceptable to them. He therefore deliberately began using the official title of *Local Schools, Local Decisions* for the devolution reforms and the *Better Schools* nomenclature was not used again in our Office. This signalled to all involved that he had taken control of the reform agenda and that he was pursuing his election commitment reforms, rather than those of Better Schools.

The Minister also needed to directly counteract the continuing push by Treasury and ERC for the LSLD goals to be efficiencies and budget savings, so he worked through the political system and had discussions with his Cabinet colleagues, in particular the Treasurer.

Because his own goals had been informed through his relationships with the key education stakeholders and were aligned around education, he knew he was on strong ground as to why the savings goal was not appropriate. He convinced the Treasurer that linking savings to LSLD would make any good management reform impossible to implement and LSLD, which was a government election commitment, would therefore not be possible to deliver. Instead, he committed to implementing LSLD with whatever money was available in the Budget. This enabled him to manage the political problem of quickly achieving ERC agreement that

LSLD would not require savings behind the school gate and should be decoupled from overall Education savings. He said of this process:

> It's an old adage that the Treasurer's job is to say no and, in my experience, they did a good job of it. Unfortunately, with education not everyone within Treasury quite understood the practical issues faced by schools. ...
>
> We had a huge fight pushing back on this savings measure. Fortunately for the government credibility in education we succeeded.

Its success was confirmed to me by the Treasurer's Chief of Staff at a meeting to discuss the Education Budget on 13 July 2011. He told me that at ERC the previous day, the Premier had said that Cabinet was "aghast" at the idea of taking money out of Education and there had been an agreement that the Department's Budget Allocation letter would include a caveat that Better Schools not be a savings measure behind the school gate.

The Minister had now achieved the alignment of the political goals of the reform with his own and those of the principals' associations. It remained only to get the two sets of goals within the Department aligned and to have a single piece of written policy advice from the Department, on which the reforms could proceed. To achieve this, we put two parallel tactics in place.

Firstly, we requested the Better Schools Taskforce to re-write BSBS as a consultation document for LSLD, focusing on what and how much authority would be devolved, rather than being an academic treatise on reform.

At the same time, our DLO Mel Marsh, who, as Liliana Mularczyk and Chris Cane both told me, had strong relationships and respect with educators, liaised with the Department and the principals' associations on the reform policies. Cane recalled that there was "lots of messy stuff" going on in the Department during July and August as the Deputy Directors-General of Schools and of Corporate Services and their staff worked closely together to identify the "main pain points (the 5-6 pillars)" as well as "getting the language right".

The incoming Director-General of the Department, Dr Michele Bruniges, was also involved even though she would not take up her role until September. She was a former NSW school principal, senior executive in Federal, State, and Territory Education Departments and held a doctorate in educational measurement. Cane said she had "deep understanding of the Department" and in August she came to a Department meeting "with reform on her mind, that dovetailed into the Minister's" and "brought different perspectives" to the process.

Cane also explained that the Department was "taking cues from the Minister's Office on the areas the Minister was interested in". They knew "he wanted the principals' groups supporting it" so the Department involved them in framing and testing the key points through including them on the internal working groups set up for each of the five key reform areas that were identified. The principals' associations appreciated their inclusion. Jim Cooper, President of the Primary Principals' Association, had thought that the Minister would focus on what the Department was telling him and keep the key stakeholders on the outside; however, they found that "the Minister's approach was totally different – he took equal notice of the stakeholders". Cooper believed this made a huge difference in the policy development process, as having practitioners tapping into any shortcomings meant the necessary changes could be made before the release of the policy rather than its being torn apart later.

This dual process resulted in two documents being sent to the Minister's Office in early August, 2011.

The first was the rewritten version of Better Schools, now titled *Local Schools, Local Decisions. Discussion Paper: Listening to communities to make good schools great*. Essentially, this was a 100-page summary of the earlier 245-page *BSBS* document which had been presented on 30 June. However, it still featured the "Flowerpot Nation" diagram, was highly theoretical, and did not contain any specific issues around which consultation might take place. The Minister wrote on his copy:

---

1   This is top down reform. Most of it is done to suit Dept/Treasury with trickle down benefits for schools.
2   This is a management consultant document. It needs to be re-written in plain English.
3   I have been briefed for 4 hours and read this document and I still don't know exactly what is being proposed.

BIG PROBLEM!!!

Fortunately, the parallel work done by the five Department working groups in the Schools Directorate had produced an entirely separate 11-page document titled simply *Local Schools, Local Decisions* (NSW Department of Education and Communities, 2011a). It said: "The NSW Government is committed to giving greater control over school decision making to principals, teachers and school communities" and described eleven reform outcomes, grouped in five key areas as follows.

Making decisions

1   Local decisions to improve teaching and learning are made by the school working with its local community.
2   The right decisions are made by people in schools and across the system, who are accountable to manage resources and deliver a quality education for all students.

Managing resources

3 Schools directly manage an increased percentage of the total education budget, including the budget for school-based staff.
4 Funding allocations to schools reflect the complexity of the school and its students.
5 Schools have the flexibility to respond to student needs by managing a single overall budget rather than many small program budgets.

Staff in our schools

6 The needs of students drive the mixture of staff, including teaching, leadership and support positions.
7 The culture of professional, quality teaching is enhanced because principals have increased local authority to make decisions about teacher performance, professional learning and program delivery.
8 Principal salary and classification are linked to school complexity, not just student numbers.

Working locally

9 Schools have more authority to make local decisions about maintenance and purchasing, including the use of local tradespeople and businesses where they offer better value.
10 Schools have more opportunities to meet their local needs by working together and combining resources (eg curriculum delivery, shared facilities, staff) within communities of schools, and across our large network of schools.

Reducing red tape

11 Schools have reduced paperwork and red tape by reporting against their own school plans instead of a complex range of separate programs.

Source: This material has been adapted/remixed/transformed/built upon from "Local Schools, Local Decisions, NSW Department of Education and Communities, 2011". © State of New South Wales (Department of Education) (unless indicated otherwise), 2023, licensed under a CC (Creative Commons) BY 4.0.

As this document had been produced in collaboration with the Minister's Office through the close involvement of DLO Mel Marsh and regular discussions with me and other staff, and it also had the support of the principals' associations, it was quickly endorsed and publicly released by the Minister on 11 August 2011. It provided the first clear statement of the agreed desired outcomes of the reform and signalled to all parties that the goals were now aligned around those of the Minister and the educators. It also marked the end of Better Schools as the Government's devolution of authority strategy with the acknowledgement that, while Treasury's requirement for overall savings in the Education Budget would need to be met, those savings would not be found in schools. Chris Cane said that this "morphing of Better Schools into LSLD created a bold reform that was palatable to the system" and there was now a clear path forward to developing its parameters and policies.

This will be detailed in the next two chapters. However, I will first discuss what was really going on during this stage of the development of LSLD and what it reveals about politicians as policy makers in large-scale education system reform.

Analytical Reflection

According to Bruns and Schneider major education reform is "almost always a highly charged and politicized process [which] depends as much or more on the politics of the reform process as the technical design of the reform" (2016, p. 5). This part of the case study of the development of LSLD provides three new insights into this aspect of large-scale system reform.

Firstly, it reveals that the *LSLD policy development process was embedded in an evolving and shifting power and political context* which manifested itself in five different goals, driven by competing ideologies. It provides insights into how the Minister used both hard and soft power, as well as politics, to gain alignment around his own goal.

The Charter Letter had formalised LSLD as a government policy which Piccoli would be expected to deliver, so the political stakes were high; but his ability and interest in using his power as a Minister to develop or influence policy was, as yet, untested. The power to determine the goals of the reform therefore lay with Treasury and the Department of Education executives working on Better Schools, which had both the authority of ERC and imprimatur of the Department to focus on delivering budget savings and efficiencies. And as the Minister did not provide any alternative policy direction regarding the inclusion of the interests of teachers and schools in the goals of LSLD for the first three months, and policy makers are inclined to adopt policy solutions that fit within the political ideology of the government (Verger, 2014), it was therefore reasonable for them to continue working towards the goals of the Treasury and ERC.

By the end of June 2011, the Minister had been in office for almost three months and was not in control of, let alone leading, the development of LSLD. The public policy process had thus far failed to satisfy the first three of Birkland's (2016) six key attributes of public policy: it is made in response to some sort of problem that requires attention, is made on the "public's" behalf, and is oriented toward a goal or desired state, such as the solution of a problem. There was no agreement as to the problem which required attention, which "publics" would benefit or what the goal should be, with three different and conflicting sets of goals in play. The Minister and his staff had to learn to understand and manage this context before they were able to gain control of the reform development process and align the various goals.

The shift in power towards the Minister really began when the "policy as text and discourse" cycle (Ball, 1990, 1994a) progressed beyond the initial process of "policy as discourse" between the Opposition politician and the stakeholders and "policy as text" as articulated in the LSLD election promise and Charter Letter.

The *BSBS* "policy as text" provided to the Minister at the end of June 2011 was the first substantive "product of the policy production process" (Ball, 1994a, p. 19) and enabled him and his staff to meaningfully engage in the policy development process for the first time. This significantly moved the process on from the three previous months of inconclusive policy discourse between the Minister, the Department, Treasury and ERC, which had served only to highlight the disparate goals of the players. It was at this point that the Minister began to lead the policy development process and use his power to manage the political context.

While BSBS did meet Shergold's[4] (2015) requirement for written policy advice to be analytically rigorous and supported by evidence, it did not align with the Minister's goals for LSLD and lacked any clear proposals around which consultation could take place. Nor did its complex diagrams and convoluted, theoretical language meet Shergold's prerequisite that good written policy advice should be both clear and reasonably succinct. It also failed to satisfy his key political criteria for good advice which "requires public servants to be sensitive to government priorities… alert to the intent and direction of policies [and] be politically astute" (p. 16). BSBS had been developed by public servants who were not educators and who had neither taken into account the election promises, nor that the political ideology of the new Minister was different from that of the previous government and of Treasury. They had not discussed these issues with Minister Piccoli or his political staff nor sought to understand his expectations.

However, it should also be noted that the Minister and his staff had, to that point, been the passive recipients of the briefings by the Department and there is no evidence that they had made clear exactly what their political intent and educational goals for the reforms were. This may partially account for why LSLD made almost no progress during the Minister's first three months in office; earlier engagement around this issue may have considerably assisted in the alignment of goals and reduced the time taken for the development of the policy.

The importance of the BSBS presentation "turning point" on 30 June 2011 was that the Minister commenced taking power over the reform and directing the discourse to align with his goals. He leveraged his political power to have the budget savings goals of LSLD dropped by the Treasurer. He used his legitimate hierarchical power to instruct the Department on his expectations regarding what the LSLD policy should address and his soft power to ensure the voices of the educators were directly engaged in developing the next iteration of the policy as text.

The completion of the political power shift to the Minister and the alignment of goals occurred with the release of the *LSLD* statement in August 2011. This new "policy as text" drew together the policy discourse that had occurred following the Better Schools document and gave a clear succinct statement of the LSLD policy for the first time. It reversed the earlier situation when the policy process had failed to satisfy the first three of Birkland's (2016) six key attributes of public policy. It now identified the problem which required attention as being how much and what authority would be devolved to schools; the "publics" to benefit would be schools, students and school communities; and the goal was to improve student outcomes by "giving the teachers and principals who work with students every day more authority to adapt what they do and how they do it to meet the needs of their students" (NSW Department of Education and Communities, 2011a, p. 3).

Secondly, *the interplay of power and politics during this period provides insights into the complexity of the systems context within which large-scale system reform is developed.*

The Minister was part of the complex broader Government political system which included other Ministers, Cabinet, ERC and Members of Parliament, with their wider election commitments and goals. The Education Department was also a complex, multi-centred system which was itself embedded in the wider educational system context and within which a range of disparate goals could and did exist, rather than being a single simple hierarchical system over which the Minister had authority.

The different approaches to the LSLD reform development process may be a result of how the various proponents viewed the system in which they were located. The ERC/Treasury/Better Schools approach reflected a tightly coupled view of the formal hierarchical power and authority relationships within the system: policy would be set at the top (through ERC) and the Minister, Department and public schools required to implement it. However, this neglected to recognise that there existed simultaneously the more loosely coupled formal and informal sets of connections and interactions between the various stakeholders, of which the Minister was also aware. There seemed to be little understanding by the Department that involving all stakeholders at all levels and in all parts of the system in the development of policy changes, rather than simply relying on the legitimate authority hierarchy, could help to address the "too-tight" versus "too-loose" conundrums faced in many governmental reforms where they struggle to find a balance between central controls with strict accountability measures and fully devolved systems with no central control (Chapman & Fullan, 2007).

This potential for a range of disparate goals to exist in various parts of the education system and the requirement for a Minister to align them through the political process is not an aspect of large-scale system reform development which has been explored in the research. For example, while Bruns and Schneider (2016) and Shrestha et al. (2019) both discuss the need to identify and analyse the interests of stakeholders, they refer only to those who are outside the organisational context of the government and the public school system and seem to assume that the interests of those within those systems will be aligned. However, as we have seen, in this case, the Minister and his Office had to constantly be aware of their position as part of a web of loosely or tightly coupled interconnected elements of a wider systems context and develop strategies to manage this appropriately.

It was only possible to achieve the alignment of the reform goals through the Minister's active use of power and engagement in the political processes related to ERC and the wider government reform agenda.

Finally, this case study provides new insights into the *role of the Minister in conceptualising and developing large-scale system reform*.

It demonstrates that Ministers are not simply the "customers of policy advice" (Washington & Mintrom, 2018); they play an essential role in policy making through handling the political strategies of public policy development (Ball, 1994a; Stewart, 1999) and by clearly articulating their policy intent (Washington, n.d.). It provides insights into how politics shapes the way in which policy is made by politicians, how they utilise soft power and how they conceptualise and operationalise their role in developing policy for large-scale system reform.

It also sheds light on how the political ideology of the Minister can play a critical role in the policy that is adopted, which Chris Cane summed up in saying:

> We were extraordinarily lucky with a National Party member as the Minister for Education, who had an appreciation of challenges faced by schools in rural locations. That can't be underestimated. If we had had a Liberal Minister then it would've been Better Schools not LSLD.

In summary, this chapter provides insights into how the political and historical context shaped the conceptualisation of LSLD, which assists our understanding of the politics of education reform (Shrestha et al., 2019). In particular, it highlights the need for ministers to ensure there is clarity of both the political and policy expectations of reform at the start of the process. It also demonstrates the importance of the minister's active role in identifying any goal conflict and providing political leadership in achieving goal alignment during the conceptualisation and development process of large-scale system reform, as failure to do so risks the failure of the reform itself.

It shows how the political context magnifies the complexity of this task, as there is the likelihood of multiple different goals which will need to be identified and resolved before reform can be progressed and there are multiple players in a complex system where the power and authority relationships are unclear or fluid. Both political and policy issues therefore need to be addressed and the use of hard and soft power by the minister, as well as good relationships with both the public servants and wider education stakeholders, are critical in doing so. These are areas where the research has so far failed to shed much light because education politics and its far-reaching consequences have not been embraced as a target of comprehensive, in-depth study (Gift & Wibbels, 2014; Moe, 2012; Moe & Wiborg, 2017).

With the goals of LSLD aligned and the statement of the 11 points it was intended to achieve agreed, the next stage of the process moved to the evolving leadership role of the Minister as a policy maker in managing the political context of the development of the LSLD policy through consultation and engagement with key stakeholders.

Notes

1 One election promise was to appoint an educator as the Director-General of Education, so the former Director-General was moved to another Department and Ms Christie was appointed as Acting Director-General while recruitment occurred.
2 Department Liaison Officers (DLOs) are staff seconded from the Department who are not permitted to engage in political matters or give political advice.
3 I am using Nye's (1990) concept of soft power as the ability to co-opt rather than coerce and hard power as the ability to command.
4 Professor Peter Shergold, AC, is an eminent academic and public servant. He was Chancellor of Western Sydney University from 2011 to 2022 and was Secretary of the Department of the Prime Minister and Cabinet from 2003 to 2008 – the most senior official in the Australian Public Service.

5
CONSULTATION AND ENGAGEMENT
Building support and managing opposition

> Cultivate relationships with teachers, parents, principals and the union, as well as with your parliamentary colleagues. Empower those who will be directly impacted by reform to speak freely and frankly to you.
>
> (Adrian Piccoli)

Once the broad parameters of the LSLD reforms had been articulated and made public, the next challenge for the Minister was to determine how much authority should be devolved to get the right balance between systemness and autonomy on each of the five reform dimensions and whether any other potential areas of decision-making should be considered. A major consultation process during the following four months informed the basis on which these decisions would be made.

The role of ministers in such consultation and engagement is contested. The public policy literature considers it to be part of the policy development process which is carried out by public servants (e.g., Althaus et al.'s (2018) policy cycle). However, the politics of education literature regards it as a vital part of managing the political context (Bruns & Schneider, 2016; Bruns et al., 2019; Moe & Wiborg, 2017; Shrestha et al., 2019). Former Education Ministers have also emphasised the importance of their role in consultation (e.g., Adonis, 2012; Andrews, 2014; Gillard, 2014). However, there do not appear to be any detailed descriptions of the processes undertaken by ministers in developing the content of the policy while simultaneously managing the political context of reform through the consultation process. DiSalvo (2017, p. 663) claims that this "huge gap in our knowledge" is a major research agenda for both scholars of education policy and political scientists, so this chapter adds to the limited existing knowledge in this area.

DOI: 10.4324/9781003515265-7

The formal consultation context

The Minister wanted to ensure that all education reforms reflected and addressed the real concerns of principals and schools. He had therefore committed to the education stakeholders that they would be involved in the development of LSLD through a thorough consultation process around how much control principals wanted and exactly what the devolution of decision-making would mean for schools and the systems that supported them. He announced this when he released the LSLD document saying: "I will be asking the incoming Director-General Dr Michele Bruniges to work with principals and other staff in the Department to consult widely in order to establish a detailed framework for making decisions to improve outcomes for students" (Piccoli, 2011).

This consultation process was one of the key issues the Minister and I discussed with Dr Bruniges when we met with her a week before she took up her appointment in September 2011. As she had been involved in the development of the 11 points, she was fully familiar with them and she quickly oversighted their transition to the *Local Schools, Local Decisions Discussion Paper* (NSW Department of Education and Communities, 2011b). This was released under her signature only three weeks later, on 19 September 2011, and the ten-week formal consultation period was commenced immediately.

It included face-to-face forums for principals, teachers, other staff and community members, a moderated online discussion forum open to all contributors and written submissions. The Minister wanted to see high levels of participation to give the consultation credibility, so he asked me to check with Dr Bruniges that the Discussion Paper had not only gone out to all teachers, but also to all public service (administrative and professional) staff working in schools and in the departmental offices, as well as to the NSW Teachers Federation and the Public Service Association (PSA)[1] and that the Department had briefed them.

In direct contrast to the previous "Better Schools" paper, the LSLD Discussion Paper was written in plain English, contained no references and was only 14 pages long. Importantly for consistency of reform messaging and for credibility with the stakeholders who had been involved in developing the 11 points with the Department, the Discussion Paper extracted the entire contents of the August LSLD document into "text boxes", then built on them by adding context about the issues and the current NSW position on each of the five reform areas. It also asked specific questions about each of them. For example, in the section on Managing Resources (NSW Department of Education and Communities, 2011b, p. 6.) it said:

Tell us what you think

- What types of resources currently managed by the state office or regions should be shifted to the school budget?
- What local factors should be used to determine funding allocations to schools?
- Which of these factors are the most important?
- How can we streamline and simplify school budgets and reporting to increase local flexibility?
- What accountability processes should be in place?

With the formal consultation process underway, the Minister could focus on his complementary political and policy consultations with key stakeholders, to which I now turn.

Engaging and consulting with education stakeholders

The Minister knew he needed to continue to understand the views and concerns of stakeholders and gain their support for the reforms during the Department's formal consultation period. He therefore undertook his own consultations with them, which were complementary to the formal process. The key feature was that he used different strategies to engage with principals and teachers in schools (where the focus was mainly on policy and operational matters), to the engagement with education stakeholder organisations (where political elements related to the proposed reforms were also in play) and to the engagement with political stakeholders (where the focus was almost entirely political). He said of this approach:

> Governments and Education Ministers pull the levers for education systems to change, but the reform agenda will falter without the support and engagement of teachers, principals and parents. It is important to listen to the many, and often conflicting, views about the right course of action.

Engaging with schools and principals

From the first week he was appointed, the Minister had held *regular meetings with school principals to gain insights into issues for schools and receive unfiltered advice on reform ideas*, saying:

> Nothing is more powerful for a Minister and nothing scarier for the bureaucracy than when Ministers get to see and inform themselves first-hand what is happening in schools. No minders, no public servants – just seeing the nitty gritty of where policy and operations intersect.
>
> Ministers need to understand that if a reform doesn't work in schools, then it doesn't work.

These meetings had initially been conducted in the traditional manner of lengthy formal tours of single schools with a thick folder of briefing papers about the school provided to the Minister, but he quickly realised this was an inefficient use of his time. Instead, we moved to a different model, of which he said:

> On most occasions we would gather a group of about a dozen, usually principals, without any other people in the room[2] and have a good off the record conversation about what they were thinking, what pressures they were under, what they needed us to do, and just as importantly what they needed us to stop doing.
>
> These were always very insightful. I am not sure the department liked me doing it because I would often find out issues before they did. It truly empowered me to test and challenge advice I was receiving from the department. I could say that advice provided to me did not accord with the conversations I was having with principals.
>
> On more than one occasion I was told in no uncertain terms that it was very unusual and not always welcome for the Minster to know more about what was going on in schools than some member of the department.
>
> It also let me take the temperature of principals and teachers on areas we were considering reforming. I could road test ideas to see if they had support from the profession which sometimes ran contrary to the view of their industrial representatives.

At these meetings, the Minister sought to gain specific examples of issues raised in the LSLD Discussion Paper that principals were dealing with in schools and where devolution of decision-making would help them achieve better outcomes for students. One which regularly arose was around the centralised purchasing policy, of which Liliana Mularczyk, President of the Secondary Principals' Council, said:

> The frustration of principals was around being shackled to operations and who you will purchase from. From local electricians to cricket balls, it was a complicated process. The Minister would ask: "Why can't you just do that?" and the principals would explain that there were ways you could get round, it but not the 'culture' to do so. This became such a desirable aspect of reform for principals to make decisions about.

As well as focusing on the content of the reforms, the Minister also heard directly from principals about what was not going so well with the formal consultation process and their concerns that the information they were providing was being filtered by the Department, saying:

> Sometimes I had to communicate our direction directly to principals and teachers because it wasn't getting there through the proper channels.

He was particularly concerned that the formal consultations were not contextualising where LSLD fitted into the overall reform agenda and he and I discussed what he wanted included in his speech to the upcoming Primary Principals' Association Conference and in any other speeches. I noted his concerns as being:

> Context – the narrative about the "enabler". It is not the end game. These things → teacher quality, better outcomes for students etc. What follows from LSLD. This is not being said in the consultations.

I raised this with Dr Bruniges to ensure that the Department speech writers then framed speech drafts around this narrative.

Similarly, when the Minister was told by principals that schools were drowning in red tape and paperwork, he followed this up by asking Dr Bruniges how many policies applied to schools. She initiated a Departmental review which found there were more than 200 such policies, including "Rocketry activities in schools" and a "Policy on school policies"; this led directly to the inclusion of "fewer, simpler policies" in the "Reducing red tape" reform area of LSLD.

In addition to these scheduled meetings at schools, Piccoli would also make unscheduled "drop-in" visits to schools when he happened to be driving past, to consult principals informally about ideas for reform as well as issues arising in education more broadly. This initially caused some consternation for both the Department and the schools, as he describes:

> I always consulted down the line, often unofficially and off the record. I often just popped in to the department or schools for a chat. That was always the best way to find out what I was not being told.
>
> Early on during a visit to Dubbo[3] I popped into one of the local high schools unannounced. Apart from the shock the Principal got when he realised who was visiting, it was a very insightful visit.

> About a month later the National Party had a conference in Broken Hill[4] to which I was intending to go. The Department heard about this so they sent a memo to every school in western NSW warning them that the Minister has a tendency to just drop into schools and that if someone comes to the front desk saying they are the Minister, then it probably is!

The Principal of the Dubbo high school was more direct and we all laughed when we heard that the Principal had tweeted other western NSW principals: "If a short bald bloke turns up saying he's the Minister and wanting to see you, he probably is!"

While the Departmental Executives were at first offended and upset by the Minister's sometimes knowing more than they did about an issue, they came to accept it. So, when he said to them "that's not what I am hearing", one of the Deputy Directors-General would smile and say ruefully: "Oh Minister, have you been visiting schools *again?*" And Dr Bruniges joked that she was going to set up an alarm system to warn her when he was inside the building.

These initiatives enabled the Minister to establish personal relationships and hold in-depth discussions with a large number of principals about many issues in education. The Minister's Diary Secretary estimated he had met with over 300 principals in schools during 2011 and this personal contact with approximately 14% of NSW school principals in nine months enabled him to be well-informed about what was happening "on the ground". He would then triangulate this information with the formal advice he received from the Department and others and ensure we were not blind-sided by potential unanticipated problems with the reforms. Also, as Mularczyk and Cane both commented, it built credibility with principals, not only for the consultation process, but also for the reforms and for the Minister himself.

Engaging with principals' organisations

As well as hearing first-hand from individual principals, a critical element of the process of reform development was *understanding the views of key education stakeholder organisations*. The Minister said:

> I understood that policy pronouncements from governments will not change anything unless they have the support of educators. We always asked educators as we were developing reforms and then checked our reform proposals with educators before we announced them to get buy in. That's why we engaged so strongly with the profession and the unions. Some teachers think they work for the union. So, the union has a lot of power to stop reform.

As we have seen, the Minister had already established good relationships with the leaders of these organisations while he was in Opposition and further developed these through including them in both formal and informal meetings when he became Minister. One of his first actions had been to invite all the key education stakeholders to discuss the upcoming Australian Ministerial Education Council which comprises all the Federal, State and Territory Government Education Ministers and was scheduled to meet on 15 April 2011, only 12 days after he was sworn in. Jim Cooper said of this:

> The meeting in the Minister's Office with all the other stakeholders just after he was sworn in, and going through the agenda of Ministerial Council, was the first time that ever happened. We felt like we were in the "inner sanctum".

The Minister also held regular formal meetings with individual principals' associations and unions and spoke at their conferences. Cane said:

> The Minister was fronting up to SPC and PPA meetings talking about the reform and backing it in. ... He was very active visiting schools…dropping in…advocating, speaking at conferences and writing OpEds…. He was consistently on message … he made it clear to the workforce this was going to happen.
>
> Because he was not 'a crash or crash through' minister he was prepared to stand up in front of groups and didn't shy away from the difficult issues. …He engaged in robust conversation and took questions.

Similarly, Mularczyk said that during the consultation period the Minister was travelling, checking and consulting with people:

> They came to the table wanting to listen, challenge and talk. He was trusting (especially of Michele Bruniges) but he also tested what he was told…You were always heard, but your voice was not the only one…. There was never a consultation forum we were not invited to or not made aware of both regionally and in Sydney.

Less traditionally, but perhaps even more importantly (and to my consternation as his Chief of Staff when he did not tell me), he often "went off the reservation" by having a casual unscheduled coffee with union and other sector leaders and educators to discuss issues and seek their views. DLO Mel Marsh said:

> A major strength, perhaps the major strength, was that Adrian led the reform *with education stakeholders*. He leveraged strongly off his relationships built from two years in Opposition. I would lose count how many breakfast meetings and conferences were had with NSWTF, PSPF, AECG[5], PPA and SPC. It really was done with the benefit of partnership.

These strategies built strong relationships between the Minister and his office and the principals' associations. Mularczyk said:

> The relationship was about *esteem* rather than *power*. He didn't portray power. He fostered discussion and consultation offering alternative views and perceptions. Principals can be conservative. He wasn't conservative and it frustrated him that they were narrow and had not thought it through.
>
> His credibility filtered through quickly to unions and across sectors and associations which fostered joint policy and practice across the sectors and transparency.
>
> His Office was also really important - not one person but everyone. This led to open consultation with his advisers as well… If there was an issue, the Minister's Office was always open to facilitating a forum or a meeting and others were given the chance to contribute.

Similarly, Cooper said:

> Co-operation between the PPA and the Minister and his Office was good during the consultation. They picked clever people to be representatives of it and always had representatives at meetings. The Minister set up the structure and allowed stakeholders to get involved which was essential …
>
> During the consultation there were meetings with the Minister and myself, our Vice-President and our Secretary – just the three of us – for him to get our opinions on issues. It happened regularly.

These ways of working became a permanent feature of the Minister's stakeholder relationships and were vital in developing and gaining support for the NSW reforms. Piccoli summarised the process and its benefits as being:

> We ensure that education in NSW is both relevant and effective through our continuing consultation with our key stakeholders. I meet with all them regularly and their input and advice has been critical in developing and implementing our reforms plus ensuring that we are continually addressing the real issues and concerns of our stakeholders. We think this is a strong, sound way to ensure quality, accountability and transparency in our reform agenda.

The submissions by principals' associations to the Department's concurrent formal consultation process also reflected their engagement with the Minister in the process of reform development.

The Secondary Principals' Council submission provided detailed responses to the Discussion Paper. It highlighted that: "It is widely recognised in schools that the need for management reform is greatest in the bureaucracy of the Department" and stated that they supported *LSLD* as an "effective enabler of reform" if there were specific actions in the areas of staffing and professional capacity, financial and management reform, and aligned local governance (NSW Secondary Principals' Council, 2011).

The Primary Principals' Association also generally supported the LSLD recommendations that would enhance student learning and school leadership, subject to the maintenance of the state-wide staffing process and the continuation of priority placements, while specifically rejecting any proposal that threatened security of tenure. According to its President, Jim Cooper, the PPA principals held discussions around LSLD and produced a paper about it which was provided to all PPA principals on 29 October 2011, with a request for feedback. He said: "Responses ... have been overwhelmingly supportive, including what PPA Principals would be prepared to support, what we would not be prepared to support and recommendations to enhance student learning and school leadership" (Cooper, 2011, December 5).

Not only did the principals' associations express their general support for LSLD, but the Parents' and Citizens' Association was also mostly favourable, with its President saying, "The Local Schools, Local Decisions looks pretty good to me"; although another P&C spokesperson was more cautious, saying that association had received mixed feedback from school communities.

However, while their engagement with the Minister during the consultation may have influenced the submissions they made, there were also other political factors at play which amplified the principals' associations' support for LSLD.

According to Maurie Mulheron, at that time the PPA was attempting to establish a "Principals' Union" and break away from the NSWTF. Cooper says this was because 95% of principals were members of the NSWTF but they represented only 3% of its membership and, when industrial matters arose in schools, the NSWTF would support the staff member and not the principal. The issue of using LSLD as politics was discussed by the PPA Council and Mulheron says that support for LSLD and characterising opposition to it as "anti-principals" was used a way of strengthening their case and differentiating them from the NSWTF.

This can be seen in the way in which Jim Cooper, as PPA President, took issue with the NSWTF for misrepresenting the PPA's position on LSLD in a trenchant letter to the NSWTF *Education Journal*, where he said:

> The NSW Primary Principals' Association is the professional association of 1800 principals across NSW, the vast majority of whom are also active members of the NSWTF. It is therefore particularly disappointing to read the extraordinary comments critical of Federation principal members by [the NSWTF] about the NSWPPA Recommendations Paper on Local Schools Local Decisions (LSLD)... It's time for some rational discourse
>
> *(Cooper, 2011, December 5)*

As we will see in the next section, this industrial conflict between the principals' associations and the union assisted the Minister in leveraging the benefits of different engagement strategies with different types of stakeholders to politically overcome the union's opposition to LSLD.

Engaging with the union

In such a context, it may appear surprising that the NSWTF did not come out more strongly against LSLD during the consultation period. As Maurie Mulheron told me, the NSWTF was opposed to the devolution of authority as an ideological attack on public education provision, and believed that it "suited the principals' interests to play it up to the Minister". However, the reason lay in the broader political context. The NSWTF was supporting a campaign by Unions NSW opposing changes to the NSW Industrial Relations Act and strike action had already occurred in September 2011. Mulheron said that was the "main game for the NSWTF leadership at that time, so LSLD consultation was on the backburner".

While that gave the Minister some breathing space, he was keenly aware that the NSWTF was the stakeholder with the most power to prevent LSLD from ever becoming policy. He knew that at some point he would need to address this issue directly and play a key role in managing it, so he firstly set about understanding them, saying:

> The Teachers' Federation is a particular beast. Historically very powerful and very militant. But as Abraham Lincoln said: "Do I not destroy my enemies when I make them my friends?"
>
> So, I set about understanding them. Understanding what their strengths were. Understanding the pressures their leaders were under from their own membership. Understanding that their leaders are also elected. Understanding the history of their organisation and why they had such poor relationships with some earlier Ministers and understanding the changing nature of their membership. I soon understood that they are a divided organisation as well.
>
> What I did learn from the very beginning was that we agree on most matters with respect to education and that we have clearly defined the things we disagree on. From the outset, we agreed that we would work together on what we agreed on and confine our disputes to what we disagree on. Most importantly we would not let these two things interfere with each other.

In addition to understanding the union, the Minister knew he also needed to proactively build and manage relationships with them and he set about doing so in a different way from that of his predecessors.

> I insisted regularly to my office and the department that we involve the unions in those matters of education reform we both agree are important. The department would often second guess me on this because of their own historic, often negative, relationship with the union.
>
> I insisted they leave the politics up to me and simply provide me with the best possible advice and consult everyone – including the union. I understood from Australian and international experience that unions working against government can sink reforms and I was intent that that would not occur.
>
> Four or five times a year I would arrange an off-the-record breakfast with senior executives of the union to discuss ongoing issues and to run some thoughts past them to take their temperature on matters. Our trust levels were very high. I provided them with involvement and trust in decision making to which they had never had access before. We allowed the union to be part of the decision making and that's something I am very proud of. We threw off the traditional adversarial relationship in the best interests of children.

Mulheron acknowledged this, saying:

To Adrian's credit he did consult and talk. There were never deals done, he was always testing ideas – not a bad thing. He would say: "If I want to do this, what would you think? Has it been tried?" Some were harebrained, but he was prepared to listen and learn.

In this wider political and industrial context, the NSWTF initially appeared to at least support the concept of devolution of authority, albeit with certain caveats. Deputy President, Gary Zadkovich, said that:

Federation supports policies that enhance the capacity of principals, teachers and schools to deliver high-quality public education. Greater school-based decision-making and principal authority are supported in the pursuit of this goal, when and where it is demonstrable that this approach neither undermines nor diminishes:

- equity and excellence for all students and schools,
- statewide curriculum, resource and staffing guarantees,

- teachers' employment rights and entitlements,
- and the primacy of the principals' role as educational leader.

(Zadkovich, 2011, August 29)

However, other views indicating at least cynicism towards LSLD were quickly expressed more openly in the Federation Journal. For example, it reported that the Minister used his opening address at the 5th Biennial Equity Conference in August 2011, "to reiterate his government's agenda of promoting so-called school autonomy" and claimed that "his persistent use of the mantra of ridding schools of so-called 'red tape' to better address school communities' means was not missed by the 1000 or so delegates" (Boutgatsas, 2011).

Zadkovich soon moved to caution that: "Increased school-based decision-making should be motivated by the pursuit of genuine educational improvement, not government cost-cutting, as outlined in the Federation's Response that has been sent to schools" (2011, October 24). However, the Federation's one-page *Response Guide to Local Schools, Local Decisions* (NSWTF, 2011, October 17) did not oppose LSLD, rather, it set out 12 brief statements, relating to each of the five reform areas. Some of these were framed as demands, such as requiring that "the statewide staffing and resource formulae *must* be maintained"; some were suggestions, such as "school based decision making *should* determine maintenance and purchasing decisions"; while others offered conditional support, for example: "Measures to reduce 'red tape', paperwork, administrative and other non-teaching tasks *are supported*, providing such measures do not negatively impact on the quality of education" (my italics).

Mulheron told me that real opposition to LSLD began when he became NSWTF President in early 2012. He said that he looked at LSLD closely and concluded that it would lead to increased casualisation and centralised cutbacks and these concerns led to an about turn by the Federation to redirect energy to LSLD. He therefore immediately went on the attack against it, claiming that both federal and state politicians saw "local autonomy" as a way to fragment the government school system and reduce funding, saying:

Let's be clear: "local schools, local decisions" is a marketing slogan, an attempt to sell a profoundly dangerous set of ideas. ... The deceit is the attempt to beguile the community into believing it is genuine reform by cloaking the real intent with weasel words like "local", "autonomy", or "self-managing"

(2012, February 13)

This sentiment was echoed by Zadkovich who claimed that the entire system of public education was at risk and called for a "strong, united political and industrial campaign" against LSLD, saying:

Devolution is the great con of school education policy around the world, and few school systems have successfully resisted it. .... Increased school-based decision making, greater school and principal autonomy … whatever it is called, the aim is the same. Governments want it, push it, and promote it, because it provides the means to cut expenditure.

(2012, February 13)

Following the announcement of the LSLD reform in March 2012, the NSWTF campaign against LSLD increased, with stop work meetings held in May 2012 and a five-week advertising campaign launched in June. It culminated in a 24-hour strike on 27 June, in defiance of an order from the NSW Industrial Relations Commission to call it off. Up to 50,000 teachers were reported by the Australian Broadcasting Commission as attending rallies across the state, forcing the closure of more than 2,000 schools (ABC News, 2012, June 27).

The strike was condemned by the Parents' and Citizens' Association, and Minister Piccoli labelled it as "belligerent and contemptuous", saying:

> I join more than a million parents today in being very angry with the teachers' union over this industrial action. No other organisation or individual can show the sort of contempt for a court order as we've seen today by the union (ABC News, 2012, June 27).

He told the media that: "The union executive feel very threatened by these reforms because it goes to the heart of the union's power" (*Sydney Morning Herald*, 2012, June 27).

However, despite Mulheron's claim that "We'll go on for as long as it takes" (*Sydney Morning Herald*, 2012, June 27), by August the union had lost the battle to defeat LSLD. While the detail of the actions of the NSWTF in opposing LSLD is outside the scope of this book, Piccoli had no doubt that his extensive formal and informal engagement with schools and principals directly, as well as with the principals' associations, was an important factor in dividing the response of the education community to LSLD, saying:

> This reform looked like it was going to get ugly. The union had declared war on it. But I knew the Principals were on side with this. I also knew that public opinion was on my side.
>
> I knew I had this battle won during a conference of the NSW Primary Principals' Association. I was asked to sit on a panel of three people: myself, the President of the PPA [Jim Cooper] and the President of the Teachers' Federation [Maurie Mulheron]. As we discussed this issue, the President of the PPA made it clear that his members liked the idea of having greater decision making whilst the President of the Federation raised his concerns that Principals couldn't be trusted to use these powers properly. The union president was reminded that 95% of

> Principals were members of his union, although Principals made up only 5% of his membership.
>
> They started to more or less argue on stage between themselves about the merits of this reform. At that moment, I knew I had it won.
>
> Had the Union and the Principal groups both opposed these reforms then we would have been in real trouble. I was very happy to have the principals on side.

Cooper also agrees that this Conference was "the turning point" where the union lost the war against LSLD because of the power of the principals' associations on the issue, saying: "It was the support from the PPA and SPC for the controversial stuff that got LSLD up. The principals were more concerned with the kids, but the Teachers Federation were concerned with the teachers".

Gavin, who has undertaken extensive research on the NSWTF, also confirms the importance of the role of the principals and their organisations in that regard, saying that:

> Resistance towards the policy [LSLD] was undermined due to divisions within the education community and conflicting views about the merit of the policy within the teaching community. ... [T]he NSWTF's message was diffused by some school principals and NSW principals' organisations praising the fact that they were being afforded greater local decision-making power, which became a source of tension between the union and principals and their professional associations during the campaign.
>
> *(2019, p. 165)*

In fact, from that time onwards there was no further industrial action and discussions with both the union and the principals' associations turned to how, not whether, LSLD would be implemented.

Engaging with politicians and government stakeholders

In addition to engaging with the education stakeholders, the Minister believed he also needed to use his power and influence to ensure that the LSLD narrative was being sold in the NSW State Government and Australian Government political contexts and that there was continued support for it by politicians.

Engagement in the State Government political context

The first part of this process was in the State Government context, where the Minister worked to build an awareness of LSLD and the formal consultations, as well as continued support for it by Ministers and government Members of Parliament.

He knew that the Department's consultation would reach into every school in NSW (and therefore into every electorate), so he requested that our Minister's Office political staff meet with the Government Whips to organise speeches about LSLD for Government Members to use in Parliament, as well as at schools and with education stakeholders in their electorates. This aspect of managing the political context is peculiar to education reform, as the majority of voters have some connection to and experience of the education system and have a view on it. This strategy therefore ensured that local Members could engage knowledgeably with their schools and communities about LSLD, thereby building credibility for themselves and for the reform.

I also consulted with the Premier's Chief of Staff on how we could further leverage the consultation process. At the next weekly meeting of all Ministers' Chiefs of Staff, he proposed that the Government "resell LSLD" by using it for a "Dorothy Dixer"[6] so the Minister could demonstrate how the Government was "delivering on its commitments and getting on with the job". This reinforced the importance of LSLD in the Government's education agenda to all the Ministers' Chiefs of Staff, and also ensured that all MPs, as well as the Press Gallery, became aware of it through Question Time.

At the same time, the Minister needed to ensure that Treasury and the Expenditure Review Committee remained supportive of the LSLD agenda and that any issues which might undermine it were addressed as they arose.

For example, the Education Department's Deputy Director-General, Corporate Services, alerted the Minister and me that the issue of having single school bank accounts (an important aspect of enabling schools to manage their own resources) had been questioned at ERC and challenged as being unnecessary, although the Premier and Treasurer were reportedly comfortable with them as a way to bring forward the enabling mechanisms required for LSLD. To ensure the significance of this issue was fully understood and that ERC remained supportive, I followed this up by meeting with the Treasurer's Chief of Staff. I explained how having school bank accounts could be used to bring forward necessary maintenance and reduce backlogs, if used in conjunction with the devolution of authority to schools to make decisions about maintenance priorities and purchasing locally. As this was a priority for Treasury, the potential ERC opposition to this measure did not eventuate.

Engagement in the Federal Government political context

The Minister also worked to manage the federal political context. This was important as NSW was already participating in the Australian Labor Government's *Smarter Schools National Partnership on Improving Teacher Quality* through the *47 Schools Pilot* which was nearing its scheduled completion when the Liberals and Nationals Government was elected in NSW in 2011. While the *47 Schools* was therefore not a pilot for LSLD, it shared some similar aims. And, as it was a Federal Labor Government initiative which had been entered into by the previous NSW State Labor Government, it gave the Minister a political opportunity to ensure that neither the Australian Government nor the NSW Opposition could easily attack the proposed LSLD policy without undermining their own reform initiative.

Minister Piccoli did this by regularly briefing the Australian Government Minister for Education, Peter Garrett, about LSLD and a range of other reform issues. He and I met with Minister Garrett and his Chief of Staff on 7 September 2011 to advise them of LSLD and the upcoming consultation process and invite them to visit one of the NSW schools in the *47 Schools Pilot* in Garrett's electorate. Minister Garrett observed that, from his national perspective, he thought that taking on local decision-making in NSW might be "hard to crack" because of the highly centralised system that had been in place for so long and because of the likely opposition of the NSWTF. To ensure the federal Government was kept informed, I continued to brief Minister Garrett's Chief of Staff and provide her with relevant documents, including when the LSLD Discussion Paper was released and when the consultation period concluded.

While it might seem an unusual strategy for a State Government Minister to brief a Federal Minister from the opposing political party about a reform proposal, it achieved its political aim of ensuring that Minister Garrett did not publicly oppose LSLD, nor attack the NSW Government politically about it, as to do so would have risked undermining his own Government's initiatives. This was a great benefit to us as, had he done so, it would have given ammunition to both the NSW Labor Opposition and also to the NSWTF which, as we have seen, was at that time already beginning to ramp up its own opposition to LSLD.

This focus on managing the State and Australian Government political contexts of the LSLD reform development at the same time as the formal consultation process *was something that only the Minister had the standing or power to do* and it had four key practical and political benefits.

Firstly, it provided a means of raising awareness of the LSLD consultations and encouraging participation, not only in schools but in the wider community.

Secondly, it enabled local members of Parliament to demonstrate that the NSW Government was delivering on its election promises in a way which would directly benefit their local communities by enabling better outcomes for students, thereby gaining their active support for both themselves and the reforms.

Thirdly, it helped to ensure that other NSW Government agencies did not undermine the Department's LSLD consultation process by pursuing conflicting agendas.

And finally, it headed off potential criticism by the Federal Labor Government, thereby depriving the Labor Party in NSW and the NSWTF of potential grounds for attack.

Analytical Reflection

The Minister played an important role in developing the content of the LSLD reform policy and managing the political context through engaging and consulting with key stakeholders. While, at first sight, this may appear to have lacked any kind of strategic approach, a clear pattern emerges when the case study is analysed using the lens of complex systems theory.

Firstly, we can see that when the Minister directly engaged with *principals*, who were public sector employees and *education system insiders*, he held legitimate authority at the apex of a simple hierarchical system. In that context, political discussions would have been inappropriate, so his engagement strategy focused on the details of what and how much authority should be devolved under the LSLD policy and on the consultation process itself.

On the other hand, his engagement with the *principals' associations* was embedded in a much more complex systems context. They were *regarded as insiders by the Department,* as shown by their inclusion in the five policy working groups developing LSLD. However, as the principals' organisations also represented the interests of principals in the political context, *they were simultaneously located within the wider education system and outside the formal structure of the Department*. Because of this complex system positioning, the Minister not only discussed the proposed content of the LSLD policy with them, he also needed to work strategically to get their buy-in to the reform process and proposals and thereby provide a political counter to the growing union opposition.

Similarly, the NSWTF's location in the education system was complex. As a registered trade union covering all NSW government school teachers the *NSWTF* was *an insider to the NSW education system*. However, it was an *outsider to the Department* and had what Mulheron described as a "hostile relationship" with it. In that context, while the formal Department consultations about policy provided a pretext for the Minister's engagement with the NSWTF, the discussions were couched in the political context as the union was opposed to LSLD ideologically, which made any detailed discussion of policy content untenable. But by treating the NSWTF executives as insiders to the education system and continuing to engage and consult with them, the Minister ensured that the relationship remained cordial and did not become adversarial until they actually took industrial action. Even then, he was careful to attack the union as an entity, not the individual executives themselves, a tactic which they also repaid in kind.

Finally, this systems theory analysis shows that the LSLD reform was also embedded in the *wider political system context* which included both state and federal government politicians. In that system, the Minister was not only *an insider but he also held legitimate authority* within it. He therefore had both the access and authority to engage and consult with the various political stakeholders to make sure LSLD met the needs of his own government and that the Opposition did not derail it at either the state or federal level. In this context, the Minister's tactics, such as using the Federal Government's ownership of the *47 Schools Pilot*, were entirely political and the policy content of LSLD was only a minor part of the engagement.

My own summary of the key new insight which emerges from this analysis of the Minister's role in the consultation and engagement process, using the lens of complex systems theory combined with the concept of system insiders and outsiders, is as follows:

As the Minister's engagement moved from being with those who were insiders in the complex education system to being with those who were outsiders, and then further out into the wider political system, it shifted from being mainly focused on policy content to being almost purely directed towards managing the political context.

This is important because a key strategy in developing large-scale education system reforms is to identify all of the actual and potential stakeholders and to analyse their interests, and the case study supports Bruns and Schneider's proposition that:

Consulting informally early and often with key stakeholders is the best way to gauge their preferences and anticipate their reactions. Crucial information in this regard is to confirm the most intense preferences and issues, that are likely to provoke opposition. Once the latter are known, stakeholders can be assessed for possible compensatory measures to overcome opposition.

(2016, p. 50)

The system conceptualisation I am putting forward here can therefore provide guidance to ministers as to what the strategic focus of the engagement with each type of key stakeholders should be. It also indicates that ministers' conceptualisation of the stakeholder universe needs to be grounded in a complex system perspective which is unique to the specific constituent elements and environmental dynamics of that particular system (Lemke & Sabelli, 2008) and so will differ in every case.

However, while politicians and political parties can be identified as important "outsider stakeholders" in this system, there is almost no literature which provides any details or insights into how ministers engage with such stakeholders or the benefits that doing so can deliver. This case study therefore provides informative examples of how ministers can both leverage support for their reform policy and manage opposition to it by tailoring their engagement with each of the stakeholders and using strategically informed and specifically targeted tactics. The benefits of this align with those identified in the literature[7] and include:

- making the case for reform, not only in schools but in the wider community and political contexts;
- generating new ideas or modifying older ones, such as reducing the number of policies applying to public schools;

- identifying areas of agreement and disagreement with key stakeholders, for example, in reforms to devolve authority for local purchases;
- building buy-in from key stakeholders, such as the principals' associations; and
- helping to smooth the path for reform by using political tactics to counter potential resistance from opposing political parties.

The case study also demonstrates the importance of having first-hand information which the Minister gained through meeting with principals and visiting schools. This enabled him to ensure that the reforms actually addressed the issues of concern to stakeholders and provided relevant examples for him to use politically to explain why the reforms were important. They also provided him with information about the consultation process itself, so that any concerns about it could be addressed and its credibility maintained.

In addition to this systems approach to understanding the Minister's role in the consultation and engagement process, this chapter adds to our extremely limited knowledge about this aspect of large-scale education system reform in three ways.

The first relates to *managing union opposition to reform*. The few political analyses of this issue emphasise the central role of teacher unions in reform politics and agree that union opposition is the pivotal issue in achieving large-scale system reform[8]. However, there is little guidance to ministers on how to manage such opposition. This case study provides some insights into the benefits of creating divisions within the education community and conflicting views about the merits of the proposed policy. It shows that one key to overcoming the union's opposition to LSLD was the strong support of the principals' associations for the reforms. As we have seen, this support had been carefully nurtured and developed by Minister Piccoli through strong formal and informal engagement with principals' associations from 2009 onwards and he was seen as unusually consultative (Stacey, 2017). It also demonstrates how a minister can use vocal opposition, such as that from the NSWTF, to strategically leverage support for the reform from other players. The political value of this approach was demonstrated when the support of the principals' associations for LSLD ultimately led to the NSWTF abandoning its campaign against it and instead moving to a rapprochement approach to achieve settlement (Gavin, 2019; Gavin et al., 2022).

However, although the Minister's leadership role in this regard was important, it is wise to issue a cautionary note here about the difference between causation and correlation. Whilst there was clearly correlation between the activities of the Minister and the outcome of LSLD, we cannot claim there is necessarily a causal relationship. We need to remember that the principals' associations and the NSWTF were also engaged in a battle of their own around whether there would be a separate new Principals' Union, and, as part of their campaign, the principals leveraged LSLD to their advantage. Also, during the consultation period, the NSWTF was not fully focused on LSLD because of the wider industrial issues that the unions were prosecuting, which also may have affected the outcome. Further research in this area will be required before a stronger linkage between the actions of the minister and their impact on managing opposition by the union can be claimed.

Secondly, the case study demonstrates *the nexus between the roles of the Minister and the Department in the consultation and engagement element of the policy development cycle.* As the case study shows, the Minister used the formal consultation being undertaken by the Department as the platform on which he built his own consultation and engagement strategy. This nexus is not well-recognised in the literature, where descriptions of policy development processes are often siloed into their academic genres. The politics of education literature focuses on the role of ministers in both formal and informal consultation; however, some of the more recent public policy development literature in Australia does not even acknowledge their role in the consultation process at all, focusing instead on the role of the public service (e.g., see Althaus et al., 2018; Ayres, 2021; Mercer et al., 2021). This case study demonstrates that ministers are not simply the passive recipients of departmental advice following the consultation process. Rather, they play an active role in handling the political strategies of public policy development which is complementary to the consultation process being undertaken by the public service.

Finally, the case study continues to demonstrate *how the policy development process moves between text and discourse.* In the previous chapter, we saw how the LSLD election promise evolved through a continuous process of moving from "policy as discourse" to "policy as text" (Ball, 1990), and back again. This chapter shows how the process of policy development again moved from the policy text of the August LSLD statement and the LSLD Discussion Paper to the discourse of further "talking about and conceptualising policy" (Ball, 1994a, p. 19) through the Minister's consultation with the stakeholders. This policy discourse was narrowed and focused by the text of the LSLD Discussion Paper, which provided a common framework and parameters within which the discourse took place and thereby ensured that practitioners, policy makers and researchers were not "simply talking past one another" (Spillane, 2013, p. 39). This also adds further depth to our understanding of "policy as discourse" as it demonstrates how the discourse around policy is both embedded in, and responsive to, the political context of the reform development and is not necessarily focused solely on the content of the policy.

This chapter shows how politicians play an essential leadership role as policy makers in large-scale education system reform development through the consultation and engagement process. It highlights the critical importance of ministers' identifying and including all relevant players and stakeholders in the process, which requires an understanding of the complex education system as a whole and its place in the wider political system.

The analysis provides new insights into how the consultation strategy shifts from being mainly focused on policy content, to being almost completely directed towards managing the political context, as the minister's engagement moves from being with insiders to outsiders, and then further out into the wider political system. It identifies the unique position of ministers as leaders in the system by demonstrating how only they have the authority and standing to consult with complete insiders about policy, and with complete outsiders about politics, and anywhere in between. It also shows how ministers can manage the political context of reform by segmenting the elements of the system and tailoring the engagement and consultation strategy with each of the stakeholders accordingly, including developing the tactics for building support and managing opposition. These aspects do not appear to have previously been identified in the literature.

Notes

1 The PSA is the union which represents public servants in diverse roles across NSW government departments, agencies and schools.
2 The group often comprised both primary and secondary school principals and sometimes included the principals of non-government schools, especially in smaller country towns.
3 A major country town in north west NSW, 400 km from Sydney.
4 A mining town in remote NSW 1,150 km west of Sydney.
5 Aboriginal Education Consultative Group.
6 A "Dorothy Dixer" is a question asked during Parliamentary Question Time by a member of the government, so the minister may give a prepared answer. All members of the House as well as journalists attend question time.
7 See Bruns and Schneider (2016), Bruns et al. (2019), Moe and Wiborg (2017) and Shrestha et al. (2019).
8 See Andrews (2014), Bruns and Luque (2015), Bruns and Schneider (2016), Bruns et al. (2019), Gillard (2014), Moe and Wiborg (2017) and Shrestha et al. (2019).

6
FROM POLICY DISCOURSE AND DATA TO POLICY TEXT AND THE ANNOUNCEMENT OF LSLD

> We clearly articulated what the situation was now, why we were changing it, what we expect it to be after the reform happens, what steps are going to occur to achieve it and when it will happen.
>
> (Adrian Piccoli)

Following the conclusion of the LSLD consultation process in December 2011, the next challenge was how to bring together the wealth of data that had been gathered during the process, with the evidence regarding large-scale system reform that was also being collected by the Department, and to translate this into the LSLD policy announcement.

While the public policy making process by public servants is well-documented, the way in which the political context impacts on the design of reform policies and the processes through which this is leveraged and managed by politicians, is under-researched (Andrews, 2017; Barber, 2015). This chapter explores this issue by describing the processes through which the Minister for Education and his Office addressed three separate but related policy and political challenges in finalising the LSLD policy. These were: ensuring the policy announcement fitted into the Government's broader political context and delivered on the LSLD election commitment; determining the policy content; and creating a document that captured the complexity of the policy in a way which was both simple and specific. While for clarity I will consider each of these issues in turn, it is important to recognise that, as the timeframe available to finalise the LSLD policy and have it ready for announcement was less than eight weeks, all the elements of the process were occurring quickly, often informally, and were not regarded nor treated by either the Minister's Office or the Department as being linear or sequential. Rather, it

DOI: 10.4324/9781003515265-8

was an iterative process and often several aspects of LSLD were being considered simultaneously.

The political context of the LSLD policy announcement

The LSLD consultation and engagement process had finished at the end of the 2011 school year and when the Minister returned from a month's leave on 16 January 2012, his first concern was *to ascertain when LSLD would be announced and how it was expected to fit into the wider policy narrative of the Government*. This was critical as it would determine the timeframe for bringing the policy discourse of the consultation together with the data and evidence into the final LSLD "policy as text" and how it would be presented. The Minister emphasised its importance to Dr Bruniges at our first meeting of the year on 18 January 2012, where we discussed priorities for the coming months.

However, while it might be expected that the timing of the announcement of a policy of such significance would be determined through a planned public policy development cycle process which was led by the Departmental policy makers and that it would be announced when it was finalised, what in fact occurred was entirely driven by the political context.

The first anniversary of the Government's election would be on 26 March 2012, and the political importance of this milestone was discussed by Ministers at the first Cabinet meeting of the year on 23 January 2012. The Premier's Chief of Staff also advised all Chiefs of Staff and Directors-General that there would be a sustained campaign of first-year celebration announcements in the two-week period leading up to the anniversary. They would highlight "what we have achieved, how we have met our commitments and what we are focusing on for next 12 months", centred around the key election themes of devolution of services, decision-making closer to the community, accountability and performance, and delivering promises.

As LSLD had been a major election campaign promise and was fully aligned with the Government's planned anniversary narrative, we knew that its announcement would be a focus for education. Its political importance in the wider Government context was made apparent when the Premier's Office advised us that the Premier and the Minister would lead off the anniversary celebrations by announcing the new LSLD policy through an exclusive "media drop" on 11 March 2012 to the *Sunday Telegraph* newspaper, which had the highest circulation of any print media newspaper in NSW at the time. This meant we had less than eight weeks to turn all of the data, evidence and information from the previous four months of discourse into a major policy document which would redefine decision-making authority in NSW public schools.

It demonstrates how the Government political context, rather than good public policy processes, drove the timing of the LSLD policy announcement and took it out of the Minister's control and also gives an insight into realities of policy making in a Minister's Office. As we shall see, this politically-driven decision not only shaped the final form and content of the policy but also led to some suboptimal policy outcomes. However, while we knew this was not an ideal process, we also knew that politically we had to fit in with the anniversary announcement schedule, so trying to delay the process was not an option. Perhaps surprisingly, the stakeholders also understood the situation and also raised no objections. Liliana Mularczyk simply saw it as an example of where: "At times you can't differentiate between policy and politics. The Minister wanted to make things better for schools through good policy, but it was also a necessity to have political announcements". Similarly, Chris Cane pragmatically recognised that: "The timing of the LSLD announcement was not great for the Department, but it was politically good and needed".

With the tight time frame and the political importance of the LSLD policy announcement established, the pressing major task was to determine what the policy would actually cover and what the process of finalising it would be.

Determining the policy

The interaction between the Minister's Office and the Department

Director-General Michele Bruniges and I both had experience as senior government policy makers and we understood and agreed that the Department and the Minister had different but complementary roles in the policy development process. The Department would undertake the public policy development role of analysing the wealth of data, submissions, research evidence and ideas that had been amassed during the consultation and engagement phase, collecting any other data they believed was required, producing reports which set out their findings and evidence for reform and drawing this together in the form of coherent and accessible information and detailed policy advice for the Minister.

By January 2012, this work was well-advanced. The Department's *Local Schools, Local Decisions: Report on the Consultation* (NSW Department of Education and Communities, 2012a) detailed the huge scale of the formal consultation process and the responses to it. A total of 444 forums had been conducted across the state, attended by 6,167 participants comprising: 1,807 principals, 1,894 teachers, 1,358 other staff, 508 students, 412 parents and 188 others. The online forum site received 3,938 visits, 312 people registered, with 198 posting 687 comments; and 4,042 written submissions were received from individuals. Every comment, idea or suggestion (over 30,000 in all) was entered separately in a purpose-built relational data base which enabled them to be tracked and filtered to assist in the analysis. The Report described the findings of the quantitative analysis of all the contributions, listing in detail common and notable suggestions for implementing the five reform directions and highlighting risks and issues raised for consideration in developing next steps.

Overall, the Report found that:

> A range of views were received in response to each discussion question, from advocates of complete decentralisation, to advocates of complete centralisation. On the whole, contributors tended to seek a greater degree of local authority than is currently available within the NSW public school education system, although they frequently emphasised the value of operating within a system.
> *(NSW Department of Education and Communities, 2012a, p. 5)*

In addition, two separate evaluations of the *47 Schools Pilot* had been undertaken. The first was the *Independent Public Review of the School Based Management Pilot* (ARTD Consultants, 2011) which was part of the LSLD election commitment and had been commissioned by the NSW Government in July, 2011. The other was Department's own evaluation which was part of the *Smarter Schools National Agreement* with the Federal Government and was budgeted at $173,000 (NSW Department of Education and Communities, 2012b). Both reports found that the principals who had participated in the *47 Schools Pilot* were overwhelmingly positive about the benefits for their school and that the vast majority wanted to have the decision-making responsibilities provided under it. The reports recommended that a number of its features might be extended to other schools and also highlighted the problems and difficulties that had been encountered. In addition, the Department's evaluation included a global review of school-based management as well as reviews of devolution reform initiatives and their evaluations in all Australian States and Territories.

These evaluations were valuable as they provided first-hand, system-relevant, contemporaneous data on the experience of principals in NSW regarding how devolution of authority actually worked in their schools and what lessons from it could feed directly into LSLD. They also provided an evidence base for the reform which the Minister discussed with Department staff, as well as with key principals from the 47 schools.

However, while the Department's policy development process seemed to imply that they would present the Minister with a formal report comprising its complete policy advice, which he and his office would then consider, this was not what actually occurred. Instead of a single, formal policy advice paper from the Department there was much informal interaction and many discussions between the Minister's Office and the public servants about the content of the policy and drafts of possible policy texts. Chris Cane described this as:

> There was lots of to-ing and fro-ing between the Minister's Office and the Department as the LSLD policy was developed.
>
> The role of the Department is to write something and recommend options and an outcome to the Minister, which leads to a discussion of the factors, which leads to good policy.

You could have those discussions with the Minister and his staff and it felt like you could trust, raise issues and challenge frankly, and have an open dialogue about them. ... It was a good relationship.

However, as this was the first major large-scale system reform policy development interaction between the Department and the Minister's Office, some of it was not as productive as it might have been as we were still establishing expectations and protocols for working together. Cane said:

It was a robust 2-way street and the feedback from the Minister's Office was direct and blunt. The Chief of Staff might listen to the discussion and say: "It's bullshit because of the political issues." But there was always the opportunity to counter without fear of being shut down. ...

There were bumps in the road and some hurt egos in the organisation around the robust feedback that was given. Some of it was overly robust and could have been toned down as some people felt alienated by it. This was more you than the Minister – you were his attack dog. [Cane was referring to myself, as Chief of Staff.]

But as it wore on, people in the Department got better at understanding expectations, and the dialogue meant the Department could draft a timetable and agenda for the reforms in a way that suited the Minister and the government's political agenda.

This provides an insight into the messy, complex, often informal nature of the process and the complementary relationship between the Minister and the Department. It contrasts with the more formal way public policy development is usually portrayed in the literature, where the Minister provides a formal sign off at the end of the process.

In our discussions, the key issues for the Minister were a mixture of policy and politics:

- What policy levers (i.e., governing instruments) needed to be moved, and how far?
- Did we have the system levers (i.e., the functional mechanisms) to implement it?
- Did the evidence provide policy and political cover?
- Did the stakeholders support it?
- How should we sell it?

The combination of these answers would determine the final form and content of LSLD.

Policy and system levers

The first and most important issue was determining what policy levers were required to address each of the eleven areas raised in the Discussion Paper and where they should be set between systemness and autonomy. Our discussions with the Department were quite explicit and I recall often using the analogy of this being similar to positioning the sliding levers on an old-fashioned stereo system between loud and soft, left and right speakers, bass and treble and so on.

The Minister's starting premise was that retaining the *status quo* of tight central control was not an option. However, he was equally clear that this was a reform to give more *authority* to schools, not to give them *autonomy*, as he had promised during the election campaign, saying: "Our *Local Schools, Local Decisions* reform is harnessing the power of the individual by giving principals more power to direct their resources while maintaining the obvious and important strengths of belonging to a large system" (Piccoli, 2014, p. 6). This recognition of the dichotomy between systemness and autonomy and getting the balance between them right was also supported by the results of the consultations (NSW Department of Education and Communities, 2012a) which, for example, indicated that:

- Schools wanted more say in appointing the staff required to meet the needs of their students, rather than having all appointments determined by State Office; *but* a state-wide staffing system was still required to enable certain types of transfers and ensure more challenging schools had excellent staff.
- Schools wanted the ability to make local purchases without having to order things centrally and to get small-scale maintenance carried out using local providers; *but* almost no principal wanted to be responsible for large-scale capital works project management.

At the same time as determining what policy levers needed to be moved and where they should be set, we also considered a number of issues relating to the system levers that were available to implement the new policy settings and how to move them.

For some of the proposed reforms, the Minister and/or Department held both the policy and system levers and they could be moved immediately; for example, permitting goods and services up to the value of $5,000 to be purchased locally. Others, such as staffing flexibility, could start as early as Term 4, 2012, but would require a gradual transition and take three to five years for full implementation. On the other hand, moving some system levers would require negotiations with other organisations. For example, many of the matters relating to staffing procedures were contained in a formal "Staffing Agreement" between the Department and the NSWTF, so a new one would have to be negotiated. This meant that, while the policy changes could be announced by the Minister, they could not be implemented until consent to change the Staffing Agreement had been reached. (These negotiations took some months and it was not until 19 September 2012 that a new Staffing Agreement incorporating the LSLD changes was reached with the NSWTF, thus allowing this system lever to be moved and the new policy implemented.)

In other cases, there were simply no system levers in existence to implement the proposed policies, so they could not be put in place until these were developed. For example, a proposed new policy to allocate more than 70% of the total public school education budget to schools (up from 10%) through providing *autonomy* would be simple – just give schools the money and let them do what they liked with it. But to give more *authority*, while still maintaining a whole system framework, an entire new funding model (system lever) would be required. A new Resource Allocation Model (the RAM) that funded schools directly and reflected both complexity and student numbers would be needed. This could not happen overnight and it would also have to be both trialled in a smaller number of schools and implemented in stages before being rolled out across the system. This led to the establishment of the "229 schools" where new LSLD initiatives were tested from 2013[1].

These considerations about policy and system levers led to our recognising that the LSLD policy would need to be far more nuanced than a simple statement of new policies regarding the devolution of authority. This understanding of the complexity of system levers and their political considerations also meant that the policy document would have to include implementation steps and timelines. Otherwise, we could see that it would lack credibility with stakeholders and be likely create significant political problems if the Minister were unable to answer questions from the media such as: "So Minister, when is this all going to happen, or it this just sometime off in the future?" The policy needed to enable him to give answers like: "It means from Day 1, Term 2 [only a few weeks after the announcement] principals will be able to purchase goods and services up to the value of $5,000 locally".

This task of developing the policy and system levers and the timelines was undertaken by the Department and then fed into the style and format of the LSLD policy documents, which I detail later in this chapter.

Evidence as politics and policy

A key issue for the Minister was to be satisfied that the proposed LSLD policy settings were supported by evidence. However, this was not just a matter of sound public policy development – it was also a matter of good politics. He said:

> Immunise yourself with evidence (this is my evidence, if you have better then show me).
> We always had a published research base behind all our decisions – we made it very clear that we were not just making things up.

There were three major components of evidence on which the Minister relied.

The first was the NSW Department of Education's *Local Schools, Local Decisions: Report on the Consultation*. This 30-page report found that contributors tended to seek more local authority than was currently available within the NSW public school system; however, they also emphasised the value of operating within a system (NSW Department of Education and Communities, 2012a).

The second was the two evaluations of the *47 Schools Pilot* (ARTD Consultants, 2011; NSW Department of Education and Communities, 2012b). The overall conclusion of the Department's evaluation was that:

> The evaluation reveals a very positive picture of how the pilot was received in participating schools and of the use of the pilot functions to create flexibility and school improvement. Most principals and other respondents said that the pilot schools had improved.
> *(NSW Department of Education and Communities, 2012b, p. 7)*

The third component was literature reviews of school-based management. The Department had already undertaken an extensive literature review as part of the development of *Better Schools, Better Services* in 2011 and drew on and broadened that review in the *Evaluation of the 47 Schools Pilot* which included a 15-page Literature Review on school-based management. This comprised a global review as well as reviews of the reform initiatives and their evaluations in all Australian States and Territories. While the Evaluation reached no definitive conclusion on the findings of the literature, the summaries of the findings of the key sources provided an overall view in favour of school-based management.

This evidence provided by the Department was then used by the Minister and his Office in two ways.

The first was to provide a strong basis for the policy content by giving direction as to the matters that should be included and where the levers should be set between systemness and autonomy. It also highlighted the problems and difficulties that had been encountered in the *47 Schools Pilot* and in other education systems, which gave guidance on the issues that would need to be considered in determining the final content of LSLD and its implementation. This was particularly helpful in informing what became the "Next Steps and Timelines" sections of the policy, with the final reforms not scheduled for implementation until 2016 – four years after their announcement.

The second use of evidence was political. Because it showed that there was widespread support for increased devolution of authority to principals, it gave the Minister a firm external foundation for the proposed LSLD reforms to which he could refer if he were questioned and also use to counter any opposition. It also enabled him to build support with stakeholders, such as the principals' associations, and assisted him to push the boundaries of the proposed policy settings in his discussions with them. He said of this process:

> Using evidence is a very powerful tool to build credibility. It is both a very useful sword and a very powerful shield.
>
> It's a very useful sword to help move reform forward in the sometimes-hostile environment of the status quo and vested interests. Change is difficult and will be strongly resisted. Evidence for why things must change proved to be the sword through which we were able to cut through much of that resistance.
>
> Having solid evidence to back up every decision is also a shield against push back and criticism.
>
> It seems flippant to say, but putting facts and evidence behind the things we did was essential to garner the support for our reforms. It seems so obvious, but in education politics and reform it is not particularly common.

For example, the Minister was able to use the positive results of the Department's extensive formal consultations as a sword to cut down the NSWTF criticisms of the *47 Schools Pilot* evaluations, which they had immediately rejected as "little more than an opinion survey and a political deceit," on the grounds the Pilot was limited to only 2% of NSW public schools which were self-selected or recommended" (NSW Teachers Federation, 2011, November 4). This assisted the Minister in the political management of the NSWTF's opposition to LSLD by demonstrating that it was ideological in nature and not based on any data. However, their intimidation of at least one principal also demonstrated to the Minister that their opposition was serious and would have to be very carefully managed[2].

At the same time, because the *47 Schools Pilot* was a trial of the Labor Government-initiated *Smarter Schools National Partnership* and not a trial of LSLD, it had the political benefit of continuing to ensure that neither the Federal Education Minister nor the NSW State Opposition Education Shadow Minister could criticise the principles on which LSLD was premised, or any proposed policies that were supported by the results of the Pilot.

Triangulation with stakeholders

At the same time as the Minister's Office was discussing the content of the LSLD policy with the Department, the Minister continued to consult with the principals' associations to ensure that they supported the proposed policy settings that were being put to him. Liliana Mularczyk said:

> The Minister required affirmation of practice or reform development ideas so he constantly tested. He had formal meetings with the SPC Senior Executive and if we said "Yes" to an idea he would test it in the field with SPC Members.

He was also doing fieldwork: visiting schools; triangulation; visiting constituents and everywhere. There was no opportunity he did not take - he wasn't using forums and initiatives as PR. He was using it to test his thinking, his Office's thinking and the Department's progress.

According to Maurie Mulheron, there was no meeting or relationship with the NSWTF from January to March 2012. However, Department Liaison Officer Mel Marsh recalls that during this period: "Adrian led many unofficial meetings with the NSWTF, and of course with the SPC and PPA". Piccoli also confirmed that he continued to include the union in these discussions and officials continued to participate, despite their publicly declared opposition to LSLD. This is consistent with my own recollections and it seems likely that, while there were no formal meetings with the NSWTF as an organisation, informal meetings with individual union officials did continue during this period.

These ongoing consultations enabled the Minister to test whether the advice from the Department on the proposed policy settings and system levers aligned with the views of the key stakeholder organisations and with those of the principals themselves and to suggest changes where that was not the case, or where braver policy settings than the Department was suggesting could be included. In particular, the support of the principals' associations gave the Minister the confidence to include some of the more controversial reforms, such teachers' salary progression based on the attainment of professional standards, even though he knew they would be opposed by the NSWTF or by the Department. Mularczyk said that this process led to principal salaries and classifications being linked to school complexity, not just student numbers, being included in LSLD, which had been a "long-held resentment with the Department". Jim Cooper agreed, saying that it was the "PPA and SPC support for the controversial stuff that got LSLD up".

Piccoli described the role of the triangulation process as:

> We double-checked the advice we were getting from the SPC and PPA by going directly to their members. I think we played a primary role in consulting directly with stakeholders to see what they actually wanted and then we played a validating role to see if what the Department was suggesting was actually what schools wanted – especially principals. We didn't split the roles deliberately, I think. That just evolved because we didn't trust that what the Department was saying was actually reflecting what principals wanted.

Creating the policy documents

At the same time that the meetings and discussions about the content of the policy were occurring, a key issue for the Minister's Office to resolve was how all of this information could be made into a document that captured the complexity of the policy in a way which was both simple and specific, and which would fit in with the first anniversary requirements of celebrating how we had delivered on the LSLD election commitment. I asked Piccoli and DLO Mel Marsh how we got from the discussions with the Department, the Minister's triangulation engagement with the stakeholders and the mass of data and evidence that we had been provided with, to the final form of the announcement and whether there was an "Aha moment" when it all fell into place.

Piccoli said:

> It came about because I thought: what was the easiest way to convey the message to the media? I imagined a two-page spread in the *Sunday Telegraph* and how they might set up an image. I imagined a "before and after" graphic, so why wouldn't we provide the content in that form?
>
> It also made it very easy for us to explain to MPs, Cabinet, and of course schools what we were doing and why it was better than what currently existed.
> Remember we always needed a "wow factor".

Marsh said:

My memory is via lots of consultation, including with the NSWTF. We [the Minister's Office] did a lot here. I spoke to the key stakeholders, as did Adrian, to see what they valued.

My memory is that Adrian knew the system was ready for reform on day 1.

If there was an "Aha moment" it was when the SPC and PPA said they would enthusiastically endorse leveraging/scaling from the 47 Schools, into the fact sheets etc.

Once the Minister had articulated the idea of the LSLD policy as "before and after" fact sheets, the work of crafting the policy statements was done by the Department. Marsh said: "The Department did the drafting for us. I recall several meetings. We asked the Department to craft the two states ['current state/future state'] so we could push for more, faster".

The issue of language was especially important in drafting the policy. As Chris Cane recalls: "There were many discussions about 'What does it mean?' and people in the Department's comms were talking to Minister's Office comms". This was not only around the words that would appear in the policy, but also in how it would be explained in the communications messaging.

One example was how the policy statement that: "Schools manage a budget that separates staffing and non-staffing funding" could be explained in simple terms. The Frequently Asked Questions document (NSW Department of Education and Communities, 2012d) would say that: "Staffing funding can only be used to engage people. Schools will be able to use non-staffing funding to support staff related initiatives as well as other resourcing needs". However, Mulheron, Mularczyk,

Cooper, Cane, Marsh, the Minister and I all clearly remember that this was better captured in the often-quoted explanation that: "You can turn a lawnmower into a staff member, but you can't turn a staff member into a lawnmower".

Mularczyk said of the importance of language in the process:

> The Minister's Office was interpreting in an accurate way what principals were asking for and using the language back to the Department.
>
> The language worked as it was the focus point. The Five Fact Sheets resonated because of the language – they were a frame, and succinct, and were planned, and brought government and everyone onto the same page. There was an understanding of what LSLD may progress to in future.

In that regard, Cane said that there was a recognition in the Department that this process of crafting the policy text was "inherently political" and the Department was "keen to make sure it met the Minister's needs" so that "when it got to the Minister it was not normal policy practice".

The final policy text of the LSLD reform, which was produced by the Department as the output of all this discourse, was anchored in the five policy areas which had been the subject of the Consultation – Managing Resources, Staff in our Schools, Working Locally, Reducing Red Tape and Making Decisions. For each area, the Department wrote a description of the "Current State" and "Future State" in short, clear phrases, which articulated the current policy settings and what the new policy settings would be under LSLD. And to take account of the fact that many of the policy settings would take some time to achieve as new system levers would have to be negotiated or developed, two sections setting out the "Next Steps" and "Timelines" were also added. Each Fact Sheet comprised only one page, so the whole LSLD policy took only five pages (NSW Department of Education and Communities, 2012c). The "Managing Resources" Fact Sheet shows this in Figure 6.1, with the complete set of Fact Sheets in the Appendix.

In addition to the Fact Sheets, the Minister's Office and the Department also put together a seven-page document entitled "Frequently Asked Questions" (NSW Department of Education and Communities, 2012d) to provide answers to both the political and practical issues and concerns that had been raised during the consultations and particularly the most contentious issues where the NSWTF was already trying to undermine the policy. The FAQs set out 27 simple questions and direct answers under each of the five areas of LSLD in the Fact Sheets and included:

> *Will school funding be cut?* No. Schools will have greater flexibility in using their funding to improve learning outcomes for their students.
>
> *Will tenure be removed for teachers?* No. Teachers will continue to have tenure when they are appointed to a permanent position.
>
> *Will nominated and service transfers still be available?* Yes. Nominated and service transfers will still be available as part of our state-wide system.

From Policy Discourse and Data to Policy Text 91

How will this improve outcomes for students? Schools will have the ability to target funding and resources at their disposal to cater for the needs of their students.

Source: This material has been adapted/remixed/transformed/built upon from "Local Schools, Local Decisions: Frequently Asked Questions asked questions". © State of New South Wales (Department of Education) (unless indicated otherwise), 2023, licensed under a CC (Creative Commons) BY 4.0

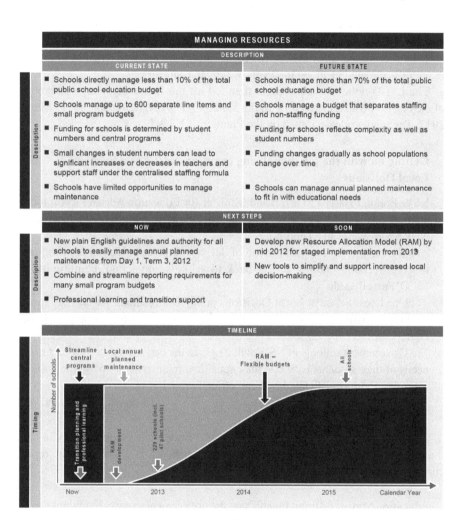

FIGURE 6.1 LSLD Fact Sheets: Managing Resources

Source: This material has been adapted/remixed/transformed/built upon from "Local Schools, Local Decisions: Fact Sheets". © State of New South Wales (Department of Education) (unless indicated otherwise), 2023, licensed under a CC (Creative Commons) BY 4.0

These two documents, totalling 12 pages, comprised the entire LSLD policy that, as we have seen, had been three years in the making.

The announcement of LSLD

The timeline for the development of the policy documents had been very tight and the political importance of the approaching deadline for the announcement of LSLD meant that I was relieved when, on the morning of 8 March 2012, Dr Bruniges telephoned me to say she was about to walk over to the Minister's Office with "multiple folders to look though – a full set of things in it". I arranged an immediate meeting for her with the Minister and our staff who had been working on LSLD to make sure all the resources, including the media release which had been drafted in our Office, could be given final approval by the Minister.

The LSLD policy announcement then led off the first anniversary celebration of the election with a media drop to the *Sunday Telegraph* newspaper on 11 March 2012. The media release issued by the Premier of NSW began:

Getting on with the job, honouring commitments: Local Schools, Local Decisions

NSW Premier Barry O'Farrell and Minister for Education Adrian Piccoli today announced the most significant and far reaching reforms to school education in New South Wales in a century.

"We are getting on with the job of delivering on our election commitment to give decision making power back to schools and school communities," Mr O'Farrell said.

"Our Local Schools, Local Decisions policy is a roadmap for change. It sets out how we will, over time, give our schools more control over local decisions," he said.

"Government schools in NSW will be given the opportunity to respond to the needs of their students based on their specific circumstances, not on the basis of formulas and forms dictated by head office."

(O'Farrell, 2012, March 11)

The headline in the *Sunday Telegraph* said "Principals to get greater say in how money spent under Adrian Piccoli's education shake-up in NSW" and the report continued:

Education Minister Adrian Piccoli said the government expects roadblocks from bureaucrats and the NSW Teachers Federation about the sweeping changes he has announced today...

"Everyone talks about how the system needs to change without actually wanting it to change," he said. "These reforms are major and they are about setting all those principals and teachers with great ideas free from the bureaucracy to try them. It's about trusting teachers again."

(Crawford, 2012, March 11)

This completed the journey of the development of the LSLD policy from its initial conceptualisation in 2009 by Adrian Piccoli as the Opposition Education Spokesman, to an election commitment in 2011, and finally to its announcement by the Premier and Minister Piccoli as the NSW Government's first major large-scale education system reform in 2012. The next stage of the policy journey would be the further design and implementation of LSLD; however, in this book, we are focused only on the process of policy development.

Perspectives on LSLD

Before considering what can be learned from the case study about politicians as policy makers in the development of large-scale system reform, it is useful to step back and listen to the voices of the Minister and the key education stakeholders as they reflect on the overall policy development process.

The education stakeholders

At the end of my interviews with each of the four Educational Leaders, I asked them to reflect on the process of the development of the LSLD policy by the Minister and his Office as they had experienced it and to consider what could be learned more broadly about the development of large-scale education system reform from it. Their views provide a unique perspective as they were all insiders to the process, and such views, together with those of the Minister and his staff, are almost entirely absent from the research (Tiernan & Weller, 2010).

I asked them to describe how they saw the role of the Minister and his Office during the development of the policy, especially *what was done well and what was not done so well*. They were unanimous in voicing their respect for the Minister because of his leadership, listening and engagement and focus on outcomes for students.

Liliana Mularczyk, President of the Secondary Principals' Council, said: "The relationship was about *esteem* rather than *power*. He didn't portray power. He fostered discussion and consultation, offering alternative views and perceptions". She also thought his leadership was critical, saying:

> He absolutely gave leadership. He was in control of the reform agenda. He forged the stage and then implementation and development went to the Department. He was the Minister that any education sector globally would want to have.
>
> He was "the Minister with principles for principals".

Jim Cooper, President of the Primary Principals' Association said: "He was the best Education Minister in 20 to 30 years because he was prepared to listen, he was not defensive and he made a difference".

Maurie Mulheron, President of the NSWTF said: "Adrian did well. He would always engage and talk and meet. There are not too many models where that happens, particularly for coalition MPs".

Chris Cane's comments summarised these views:

> He was probably the best Minister I worked for in my time as a public servant. He was prepared to listen, prepared to engage, prepared to learn. He was prepared to tell us when he was happy or unhappy, in direct terms.
>
> His leadership and commitment to bold reform based on open engaging was invaluable. He knew what he wanted and could articulate it.
>
> The Premier, Minister and DG were all focused on: "How are we going to make the education system in NSW better?" It worked past the politics and was focused on the best interests of students.

The interviewees also said a strong Minister's Office, which had good relationships with the Department and key stakeholders, played an important part in the reform development process. Mularczyk said: "If there was an issue, the Minister's Office was always open to facilitating a forum or a meeting… I have never felt so welcomed and listened to by a Minister and also his entire staff".

Cane said:

> You could have open dialogue with the Minister and the staff. The Department staff were never prohibited from engaging with advisers, including the Chief of Staff, which had happened under some previous Ministers. It was two-way, being able to speak informally to the Minister's Office, not just in formal meetings. This only flows from being open to establish a relationship and building trust. The senior DLOs became a very useful resource for the Minister and the Department and the role of Mel Marsh was a pivotal part of the mix of the relationship between the Minister's Office and the Department.

However, Cane also said that although "nothing went seriously wrong from the Minister's Office, it came across as being quite hostile at times". This was because, while its "capacity to have robust exchanges led to things getting better", it was also "a distraction and potentially a delay in doing work by some people because of their reactions". In particular, Cane was critical of one policy adviser who did not have a background in large-scale education systems and was "unhelpful during this period because of his narrow perspective".

In reflecting on what was not done well, all four key stakeholders focused on a number of failures in the implementation process for LSLD.

Cane said:

Mistakes were made in policy formulation and in implementation. The technology didn't move with the reform and [the IT reporting system] wasn't ready. I don't think we got things wrong, but we didn't prepare schools well enough or give them the skill sets to utilise the reforms. Having the 229 schools scattered across the state rather than being grouped made it harder to do that.

Cooper agreed that schools were not properly prepared, saying:

There was not enough training for principals to take on the new roles which led to some poor decisions regarding financing and staffing. The increase in workload was underestimated by both the PPA and the Minister's Office. The PPA didn't understand level of responsibility and the Department underestimated responsibility, so the bureaucracy pushed responsibility for problems onto the principals.

Mularczyk saw the timeframe for the implementation process as being a major reason for problems, saying:

The implementation process took so long and became unhealthy. Unfortunately, the bureaucrats got back in charge and the Department was getting around the intention of the Minister and the LSLD policy.

It needed an implementation Czar to have oversight of the implementation and accurately communicate that to the Minister's Office.

Finally, I asked the four interviewees what advice they would give to a new Minister about developing large-scale education system reform as a result of their experience with LSLD. It was surprisingly similar.

Mulheron said: "Trust the profession and consult widely. Try to set up mechanisms to hear the things you need to hear. Large-scale system reform won't work without professionals being closely involved in the development of it."

Mularczyk said: "Get everyone round the table and seek a truth that works, rather than consensus."

Cooper said: "Trust the principals. If you have no educational credentials, assume you know nothing."

And Cane said: "Listen before you act. Listen to people in the place and to stakeholders – the Teachers Federation, principals and others in the place, as well as to the Department. Then form a view."

The Minister

I also asked Piccoli what he thought he and his Office had done well and not done so well. He said one of the things we did well was to change some of the elements of the LSLD election promise to make sure it reflected the evidence that was provided to us by researchers and the Department, as well as responding to the concerns of the stakeholders, rather than sticking doggedly to it just because it was a policy commitment. He said:

> It's important to note that governments can get locked in to bad policy when they make pre-election announcements. You will see that what we promised is not exactly what we delivered so we didn't get locked in. Instead, we sought advice and altered what we delivered.

He also focused on "the failure to actively shape and monitor LSLD's implementation so that it remained true to the 11 policy principles" as a key problem. Interestingly, he also suggested something along the lines of Mularczyk's proposed "Implementation Czar", modelled on the recent appointment of a Fire Services Implementation Monitor in Victoria, who was responsible for monitoring the large-scale reforms of fire services. He agreed that it is essential to listen to, respect and learn from a broad range of people engaged in the process, saying:

> Recognise that no-one knows everything. Road test with everyone all the advice you are given, not only by the Department, but also by the key stakeholders and the principals. Take the profession with you in a positive, inclusive and constructive way.

What is most notable about these reflections by key insiders to the process is how consistently they identify *three key lessons*:

1. The Minister's engaging with and listening to all of the stakeholders through the entire reform development process and making sure all views are considered and tested is the key to getting the policy content right as well as managing the political context.
2. Strong relationships between the Minister and his Office with the stakeholders as well as with the Department support this process. As the comments

from the educational leaders show, the Minister and I did not always get this right.
3 It is essential for the Minister to actively shape how the policy will be implemented and how this will be monitored as part of the design process.

Analytical Reflection

This chapter provides four new insights into the role of politicians as policy makers.

Firstly, it shows how *the political context drove both the form and content of the LSLD policy documents*, which was not always beneficial.

In contrast to the five months it took for the goals of LSLD to be agreed, and the further four months of consultation and engagement with stakeholders around what should be included in the policy, the development of the final LSLD policy document itself took only eight weeks. This was due to the timing and arrangements for its announcement being driven by political considerations rather than as part of a planned public policy development process. The high-stakes political context also shaped the form and content of the policy documents because the Minister needed to be able to easily explain it to the media and sell it politically (including overcoming any opposition to it). This resulted in the entire LSLD policy consisting of five one-page Fact Sheets, supported by a set of FAQs and the Report on the Consultation, rather than being a more comprehensive policy document. This process exemplifies what Edwards et al. describe as "the paramount importance of politics in determining whether policy progresses from stage to stage and at what pace" (2001, p. 184; also Edwards, 2021).

However, Shergold (2015) cautions that policy development which is rushed because of political reasons for announcement can result in poor consequences. In relation to LSLD, it is likely to have contributed to the fact that the core policy documentation did not contain explicit steps or mechanisms by which schools were expected to achieve specific student outcomes (Centre for Education Statistics and Evaluation, 2020). This meant it did not meet Shergold's requirement that: "Execution should be built into policy design rather than treated as an afterthought" (2015, p. 17). All the Educational Leaders interviewed for this research, as well as the Minister, considered that the failure to properly plan, manage and monitor the implementation of LSLD was its major weakness, so the detrimental impact of a rushed timeline for political reasons, should not be underestimated.

A further problem with the content of the policy document was that it failed to answer one of the four key questions which Gilding claims need to be answered by policy makers: "What does success look like?" (2021, p. 246). Consequently, while it was relatively simple to ascertain that each of the five reform areas of the LSLD policy had been fully implemented in all NSW Government schools by 2018 (Centre for Education Statistics and Evaluation, 2018, 2020; Gavin & Stacey, 2022), it has also made any evaluation of its success, or otherwise, difficult.

While the evaluation of LSLD is beyond the scope of this book, it is worth noting that the evaluation conducted by CESE (from 2016 to 2020) had to assume that its overall aim was to improve student outcomes and therefore selected a range of educationally relevant academic and non-academic outcomes that they believed might reasonably be considered to show changes if the LSLD reform were successful, while acknowledging that "LSLD was implemented at the same time as many other changes were occurring across schools, meaning that it is difficult to attribute changes solely to the impact of LSLD" (Centre for Education Statistics and Evaluation, 2020, p. 9). This might have been avoided, and a more robust evaluation enabled, if a policy process which was not driven by political expectations and deadlines had occurred.

Secondly, it provides insights into how the *Minister for Education and his Office played an active, formal and informal, complementary and collaborative role to that of the public servants in the final stages of the LSLD policy development.*

As we saw in Chapter 2, the literature on public policy development generally focuses on the formal roles of public servants and ministers, which it portrays in a linear and segmented way. For example, Shergold says: "It is up to ministers, not officials, to make policy decisions … The important role of senior public servants is to ensure that Cabinet ministers make their decisions with eyes wide open" (2015, p. 5). Similarly, Washington and Mintrom see ministers only as the "customers of policy advice" (2018, p. 33). This gives the impression that it is the public servants who take the active role in identifying risks and issues and the impact the decisions will have and providing formal written policy advice, while the Minister and his Office are merely its passive recipients.

However, other researchers and authors recognise the role of politicians in policy making and how it differs from that of public servants. Stewart's important Australian work (1999) focused on what governments can do (the strategic/policy tasks) and how they can do it (their accountability/operational responsibilities), while Ball's (1994a) five contexts of the policy process include political strategies. Luetjens et al. (2019) also recognise that politicians have a role in large-scale system reform, with the majority of their case studies of successful public policy in Australia and New Zealand demonstrating the importance of the relationships between the political and public service systems. In that regard, Washington (n.d.) insightfully states that:

> Ministers … need to know how to ask the right questions and be able to articulate their policy intent; they don't have to have all the answers, but they do need to know what they want to achieve and be open to different options for getting there.

These studies provide theoretical conceptualisations of the role of governments and ministers in public policy making and also demonstrate that in many instances ministers do play a role in the process. However, they do not agree as to what that role might be and nor do they give detailed insights into how politicians themselves conceptualise and operationalise their role in developing policy for large-scale system reform.

This case study demonstrates that the development of policy is not always simply the province of public servants and that Minister and the Department played differing but complementary roles. It shows that, while the Department undertook the roles described by Shergold, there was no single formal "policy advice" document provided for consideration and acceptance by the Minister. Instead, there was what Shergold describes as "an iterative process of argument, counter-argument, negotiation and compromise" (2015, p. iv) where the Minister and his staff took an active role in challenging assumptions and evidence, adducing other ideas and viewpoints gained through the Minister's ongoing consultation and triangulation process with stakeholders, and feeding in the political considerations which would need to be addressed in framing the policy. These included dealing with mounting opposition from the NSWTF, leveraging the support of the principals' associations to include some of the more controversial reforms and considering whether the politics of moving the required system levers to implement the policy could be managed.

This process of "policy as discourse" (Ball, 1990) led to the production of policy drafts, developed in real time by email and text message communication between the Department and the Minister's Office, which did not emerge in the final form of "policy as text" (Ball, 1990) until the very end of the process, three days before the policy was announced. This aptly described "policy dance" (Bridgman & Davis, 2000, p. 31) between the Minister and his Office and the public servants is not well-documented in the academic literature (as discussed by Andrews, 2018) although some Ministers (e.g., Gillard, 2014) have written anecdotally about their experiences. The insights into the details of the "dance", especially in regard to the politics of policy making, therefore contribute to our understanding of the role of politicians as policy makers in the development of large-scale system reform policy.

Thirdly, this case study provides new insights into *how Ministers can use evidence both to underpin policy development as well as to manage the political context of reform.*

While the importance of the collection and analysis of data and evidence by public servants is recognised as an essential step in the public policy cycle (Althaus et al., 2018; Luetjens et al., 2019; Shergold, 2015), there is some debate on the role evidence plays in policy considerations by Ministers.

Former Welsh Minister for Education, Leighton Andrews (2017) claims that some have argued that evidence has a limited role in debate and public policy and asserts that former UK Secretary of State for Education Michael Gove's claim that people "have had enough of experts" could be seen as proof that that Ministers are not interested in it. Andrews maintains that in fact Ministers are open to evidence and the lack of engagement is a myth, saying that: "understanding of the routines through which Ministers work and assimilate evidence is actually under-researched" (2017, p. 1). He argues that there are three reasons why the myth persists: that the process of policy making is not well understood; the political science literature has little to say about what ministers actually do; and there is little in the literature on government about how policy change is carried through to delivery. He reflects on his own experience and claims three key factors affect the ability or willingness of Ministers to consider evidence: the time constraints under which a Minister operates; the availability of trusted sources of evidence; and the authorising environment within which the policy is being developed.

While this may well be true, it also appears to take a justificationist stance in explaining why ministers may appear to be uninterested in evidence, so an alternative might be to consider ways in which other policy makers suggest ministers might use it in the development of large-scale system reform and then review the findings of this case study against them.

At one end of the spectrum is what Kisby (2011) says is the policy neutral view of evidence presented by former UK Secretary of State for Education and Employment, David Blunkett, as: "Simple common sense, as if the facts relating to a given, objective public policy problem simply await discovery and that, once discovered, neutral policy proposals can be formulated that address the problem", and of which Kisby claims "the neutrality implied by Blunkett is bogus" (2011, p. 109).

At the other end is the entirely political view of former senior Australian public servant and public policy expert, Meredith Edwards, who opines, somewhat cynically, that:

> Once ministers have decided what they want to do – as a consequence of their political values and/or pressure from their electors or party supporters – they will seek evidence to support their decision so that they can justify the policy in public. Often what is sought, therefore, is more "policy-influenced evidence" or "values-influenced evidence" rather than evidence-influenced policy.
>
> *(2021, p. 173)*

And perhaps in the middle is the more practical view of the use of evidence by Shrestha et al. (2019, p. 8) who found it could "drive communication strategies, be used to make the argument for reforms, and gain the support of key actors, including the public" and that "an effective communication strategy could also counter the spread of misinformation by groups who oppose the reform".

These four approaches to the importance of evidence all seem to subscribe to Andreas Schleicher's tagline that "Without data, you are just another person with an opinion" (n.d.), and that, in fact, the argument is not about whether evidence is important but how it is used. This case study demonstrates that each of these factors played some part in the use of evidence by Minister Piccoli in developing the LSLD policy. However, focusing on either the policy, or the politics or the practical uses of evidence fails to recognise the complexity of how he used both a political lens as well a policy lens simultaneously on all aspects of the evidence. This ensured it was both a "sword" (LSLD was likely to be considered as "evidence-based policy" and the evidence could be used to drive communication strategies and gain the support of key stakeholders) and a "shield" (LSLD could be justified publicly and the evidence used to counter those who opposed it).

The case study therefore adds to our understanding of this under-researched aspect of the process of the development of large-scale system reform (Andrews, 2017) and which Barber (2015) has described as "the gaping hole" in this area of knowledge.

Finally, the case study shows that not only is *consultation* important in assisting ministers to make political decisions, it *is also highly valued by all the stakeholders during the design phase of the process.*

Consultation with stakeholders is generally regarded as the phase of the policy cycle which occurs prior to the design phase (e.g., see The Australian Policy Cycle, Althaus et al., 2018); however, there is increasing recognition that continued engagement with stakeholders during the design phase itself may also be beneficial. Edwards notes that "Who to consult, why, when in the policy process and how, are critical process issues" (2021, p. 174), while research by Shrestha et al. showed that "a consultative approach to designing reforms, by involving various actors in education and across administrative sectors, is likely to build support at time of implementation" (2019, p. 47). In particular, consultation with unions during the design phase is a major issue, and the decision on whether or not to do so varies enormously across countries depending on a range of factors (Bruns & Schneider, 2016).

Knowledge of what this means for politicians has been lacking until recently, when some former Education Ministers have commented on how consultation during the policy design phase can help ministers to make political decisions about whether to be braver than the public servants might be advising and to push further with reforms (Adonis, 2012; Andrews, 2014), or cause a minister to change or withdraw planned elements of the policy design rather than risk political embarrassment or even defeat (Gillard, 2014).

Minister Piccoli's continuing consultations with all stakeholders provided him with information he needed to make critical political judgements which balanced the support of the principals' associations against the opposition of the NSWTF in deciding whether he should endorse controversial issues being included in the reforms, particularly when advice from the Department was more conservative than the information he was gaining through the consultations. His continued engagement with all stakeholders during the design phase therefore led to the inclusion of important reforms which may otherwise have been omitted. This aligns with

Adonis' contention that Ministers should: "Be bold, but go with the grain as far as possible" (2012, p. 242).

In summary, this chapter demonstrates that large-scale system reform "depends as much or more on the politics of the reform process as it does on the technical design of the reform" (Bruns & Schneider, 2016, p. 5). It provides new insights into how the political context can shape the final form and content of the policy and how this can override the public policy process and lead to results which may not be entirely beneficial. It shows that policy development does not necessarily adhere to the formal cycles depicted in the literature and provides insights into the messy, complex, intricate process of the "policy dance" that occurs between with Minister and the public servants in developing the detailed content of the policy. It also provides insights into the active, formal and informal, collaborative role the Minister and his Office played in the shaping both the form and content of the policy and illustrates the political, policy and practical uses that politicians are able to make of evidence in developing reforms. Finally, it demonstrates the value of the Minister continuing consultation with key stakeholders during the policy design phase, not only in relation to informing both the policy language and content, but also regarding the political considerations as to what should be included and where boundaries can be pushed.

Notes

1. The "229" comprised approximately 10% of NSW public schools which were already participating in the Federal Government's *Empowering Local Schools* reform and included those that had been involved in the *47 Schools Pilot*.
2. One principal interviewed for the evaluation said the NSWTF had encouraged teachers to vote against the school's participation in the pilot and the Federation had instigated legal action over the claims (ARTD Consultants, 2011, p. 12).

PART III
Politics, policy, processes and people in educational change

PART III

7
UNDERSTANDING THE ROLE OF POLITICIANS AS POLICY MAKERS

> Stay on top of reform development and implementation and preferably in front of it. Reform is not a firework; it's a multi stage rocket with each stage propelling the next. Just saying it won't make it so.
>
> (Adrian Piccoli)

We have now peered inside the "black box" of policy development to see how the NSW Education Minister, Adrian Piccoli, conceptualised and developed one large-scale education system reform, *Local Schools, Local Decisions* (LSLD). Together with the Analytical Reflection in each chapter, this provided a number of insights into what politicians actually do. However, the case study alone does not give us an appreciation of the key features of role of politicians as policy makers, how policy, politics, processes and people interrelate in developing whole system reforms and why an understanding of this matters for school improvement.

In this final part, I identify the key themes that arise from the case study and then reflect on them to develop some practical strategic frameworks and guiding principles which may be useful for policy makers in developing large-scale system reforms in other contexts or jurisdictions.

To explore this, it is firstly helpful to bring together the LSLD policy making process in a table which summarises the timeline of key events, identifies who was leading it, what stakeholder engagement was occurring and its focus at each stage (Table 7.1).

With this framework as the basis, I have used reflexive thematic analysis (Braun & Clarke, 2006, 2013), to draw together the insights and the initial themes from the case study to conceptualise eight overarching themes, each united by a central concept or idea. These themes thread through and across the case study as a

TABLE 7.1 Summary of the *Local Schools, Local Decisions* policy making process.

Timeline	Events/processes	Leader	Minister's key stakeholder engagement	Focus
2009–2010	Conceptualising the LSLD reform	Shadow Minister	Union, principals' associations	*Discourse*
Early 2011	Coalition policy on LSLD released	Shadow Minister		*Text*
March–April 2011	Liberals/Nationals elected. Charter Letter sets out LSLD reform expectations.	Premier		*Text*
April–June 2011	Encountering competing reform goals	No clear leadership	Treasury, ERC, Department's Better Schools Taskforce	*Discourse*
July–August 2011	Aligning competing reform goals	Minister	Treasurer, Department's Schools Directorate, union, principals' associations	*Discourse*
11 August 2011	Minister releases LSLD document setting out 11 desired reform outcomes	Minister		*Text*
August–September 2011	Formal consultation document drafted	Director-General	Department, principals' associations	*Discourse*
19 September 2011	Consultation paper released	Director-General		*Text*
September–December 2011	LSLD Consultation	Minister (stakeholder engagement) Director-General (formal process)	Department, schools, principals, principals' associations, union, politicians, State and Federal Governments	*Discourse*
December 2011 - March 2012	Determining the LSLD policy	Minister, Director-General	Department, principals' associations	*Discourse and Text*
11 March 2012	Announcement of LSLD: the Five Fact Sheets	Premier, Minister		*Text*

whole and can be characterised as the key features of the process by which politicians as policy makers conceptualise, initiate and develop whole system reform. However, I also want to make sure these themes remain deeply grounded in the insider experience of politicians as policy makers, so I set the scene for each theme by directly quoting Adrian Piccoli on it.

Theme 1: The importance of the political context

> Education is perhaps the most political of all portfolios: it reaches into the homes of almost every voter in this State and this country.
>
> Adrian Piccoli

The first overarching theme is the importance of the political context. The case study reveals the large number and range of stakeholders, with an assortment of vested political interests, who needed to be engaged with during the reform development process. They comprised not only the teachers' union, principals' associations and interest and advocacy groups of various kinds but also a great number and range of political stakeholders which included: Cabinet and Cabinet committees; the Premier and State government ministers (22 in NSW at that time) and their offices; government backbenchers (another 88); Opposition shadow ministers and members of parliament; and relevant Federal Government ministers and their offices. This is much more extensive than those generally identified in the literature, for example, by Goldspink (2007) in his concept of the complex education system, or recognised in Bruns et al.'s (2019) list of potential political protagonists.

The case study demonstrates that for ministers, policy making takes place in the political context of government and the challenge of improving education quality therefore faces significant political complexities. It exemplifies former Welsh Minister for Education, Leighton Andrews' experience that: "Ministerial decisions are not taken in a vacuum. ... They are situated within a context defined by government commitments, a party programme, a history of prior policies, a balance of power within a Cabinet, ... and a budgetary framework" (2018, pp. 5–6).

It also shows how the demands of the political environment can impact on both the form and content of the policy and thereby distort the more usual public policy development cycle process, which may be detrimental to the policy itself. We saw how political considerations informed the initial election promise for LSLD and how the competing goals of the reforms were also premised on historical and political factors. Most significantly, the political context of the first anniversary of the Government's election drove the timing and arrangements for the announcement of LSLD. This resulted in the entire policy consisting of only five one-page Fact Sheets which omitted to deal with any implementation aspects, rather than being a more comprehensive policy document. This was seen as the greatest failure of the LSLD policy by the Minister, education stakeholders and subsequent evaluations.

As a result, Adrian Piccoli has warned:

> *Don't let the political cycle run policy reform. Stop policy by press release. Where this isn't possible, pay close attention to the policy details to make sure they do not become compromised.*

This importance of contextual factors is consistent with recent politics of education literature which finds that the design of public policy is embedded in a political task environment and that all public policy making is geared towards the single purpose of achieving governmental objectives, whatever they may be (Birkland, 2016; Virani, 2019). Politics also determines whether, and how fast, policy progresses from stage to stage (Edwards, 2021; Edwards et al., 2001) as sooner or later the intellectual debate about policy is cut off by political decisions in which politicians take responsibility for the choice of a particular problem definition and its solutions (Hoppe, 2018). This means that major education reform is almost always a highly charged and politicised process. As we saw with LSLD, what gets implemented – and its impact – depends as much or more on the politics of the reform process as on the technical design of the reform (Bruns & Schneider, 2016).

As an insider to the process, while I know that the political context is important, I was surprised to find that its scope and scale appeared much greater when viewed through the more objective lens of this case study, rather than that of my lived experience, in three respects. Firstly, I had not appreciated that managing the political context was such *a key aspect of every stage of the reform development process*, from its initial conceptualisation, as shown in how Piccoli began engaging with the union and principals' associations while Opposition Education Spokesperson, through to the announcement of the policy, which was a political "event". As this can only be undertaken by the minister and the political staff, it is a critical and ongoing part of their role in policy development. Secondly, I was surprised by the *sheer number and range of players in the political context* that the minister's office must deal with continually. Finally, I had not fully appreciated how the exigencies of the political context can significantly *affect the policy process to its detriment*, and that the minister needs to be alert to this and mitigate any impact early in the process.

Together, these insights emphasise the importance of ensuring that ministers and their staff have a deep understanding of the political context and the various complex factors at play and that strategies for managing them are prioritised as part of the process. This is a particular challenge in ministers' offices where it is often difficult to balance the urgency of the daily short-term political cycle with the importance of achieving the longer-term significant policy outcomes.

This theme is significant because it demonstrates how the political context impacts on the entire process of large-scale education system reform development and therefore influences the way in which ministers undertake their policy making role. It also provides examples of issues that need to be taken into consideration by ministers and their offices, as well as strategies that they can use to manage them.

Theme 2: Engagement with key education stakeholders

> Change will only come if the profession is on board with the reforms in a positive, inclusive and constructive way. A constructive relationship involves getting ideas for improvement from the profession themselves, supporting the work of the profession, but then engaging them in the design and implementation of reform.
>
> Adrian Piccoli

This theme relates to the Minister's consultation and engagement with the key education stakeholders who included principals and teachers, as well as principals' associations and the union.

This was not simply a one-off event which occurred as a formal part of the policy cycle. Instead, the Minister regarded his engagement activities as being complementary to, rather than separate from, the formal consultations being undertaken by the Department; his were largely informal and included the political stakeholders whose views were important, but with whom it would not have been appropriate for the Department to engage. His continual formal and informal engagement with a wide range of stakeholders was the key feature of every stage of the policy development process including:

- The initial conceptualisation of LSLD as an election promise.
- Achieving the alignment of goals between educators, public servants and politicians.
- Providing additional input during the formal consultation process through acquiring examples directly from principals in schools.
- Triangulating proposed policy settings by testing them with the principals' associations, principals and teachers during the design phase.

This is consistent with recent politics of education case studies which all found that governments which are most effective in introducing and sustaining large-scale education system reforms undertake strategic and broad-based consultations to analyse the interests of all stakeholders, gain the buy-in of those who will be vital for introducing and implementing the reform and are able to divide opponents and mobilise sympathizers where necessary (Bruns & Schneider, 2016; Bruns et al., 2019;

Shrestha et al., 2019). However, that research provides little guidance as to the role of ministers in this process or the tactics they might use.

The case study provides new insights into the process through which the Minister segmented the stakeholders in the education system, including advocates, supporters and opponents, and tailored the engagement and consultation strategy with each group accordingly so they could be balanced or used against each other, as occurred with the NSWTF. In that regard, the literature is equivocal about whether and when unions should be included in the consultation (e.g., Bruns & Schneider, 2016). However, ministers generally agree that it is critical to listen to dissident voices (e.g., Andrews, 2014) and Piccoli said:

> *Triangulate advice – trust but verify.* Do not become captive to any single source of advice. Listen to the many, and often conflicting, views about the right course of action – your adversaries often have some of the best ideas. Consult down the line and off the record.

The case study demonstrates that a key feature of every stage of the policy development and design process was ongoing formal and informal engagement by the Minister with all education stakeholders, regardless of whether they were supporters or opponents, and shows that this was a much longer, deeper and more engaged process than appears to have been previously explored, other than by former ministers such as Andrews.

This theme is significant as it highlights the critical importance of the Minister's role in identifying and including all relevant players and stakeholders in consultations throughout the entire policy development cycle, which requires an understanding of both the education system as a whole and its place in the wider political system. However, the lack of detailed research in this area represents a "huge gap in our knowledge" in relation to education system policy reform (DiSalvo, 2017, p. 663) as it means that ministers do not have any guidance on how to do this and, indeed, may not even know it is part of their role.

Theme 3: The Minister's relationship with the Department

> Pursue a collaborative and positive relationship with your department when developing and implementing policy. You don't have to agree all the time, but you do need to trust each other in the pursuit of that shared goal.
>
> Adrian Piccoli

The third theme relates to the relationship between the Minister and his Office and the Department in the design and development of the reform. The case study shows that this was somewhat fragmented during the first four months after the election. This was reflected in the way in which different sections of the Department were pursuing different goals for LSLD, with the Corporate Services Directorate focused on savings and efficiencies, while the Schools Directorate was focused on the needs of students and schools, and how the Minister's Office had to manage the process of achieving goal alignment. The Minister said of this:

> Initially the Department sanitised a lot of advice they gave me because they presumed we wouldn't go for it because of what they perceived as the political or stakeholder ramifications. I told them to stop second guessing me as they didn't know what we could or couldn't achieve.
>
> I insisted that they provide the best educational advice and that I would then assess what we could deliver through Cabinet, Parliament and stakeholders. I was almost always right. I pushed the Department to do a lot more than they were comfortable doing because I understood the political risks better than they did.
>
> I constantly reminded them that I am the politician, they provide advice and run the operational side.

However, following the appointment of Dr Bruniges as Director-General, the Minister and his Office developed a complementary, collaborative relationship with the public servants rather than primarily engaging in a formal process of briefings and decisions. The Minister set the strategic direction in line with the broad direction of the Government and he and his Office sought to develop and sustain a relationship based on mutual trust and respect, where the public servants told him what he needed to know, not what they thought he wanted to hear.

The Department and the Minister's Office then worked together through the "policy dance" (Bridgman & Davis, 2000), described by Shergold (2015, p. iv) as "an iterative process of argument, counter-argument, negotiation and compromise", to develop the LSLD policy itself. The Minister and his staff took an active role in this "policy dance" through challenging assumptions and evidence presented by the Department, adducing other ideas and viewpoints gained through the Minister's ongoing consultation and triangulation process with stakeholders and feeding in the political considerations which needed to be addressed, such the requirement for the policy announcement to further the Government's first anniversary political narrative. This is significant as it enabled both parties to use their skills, abilities, resources and positions in the system to their best advantage, reflecting the fact that "ministers (and their staff) are wide, but [public service] officials are deep" (Hollway, 1996, p. 136).

However, this element of large-scale system reform is not well-documented in the literature on public policy development which generally focuses on the formal roles of public servants and, to a lesser extent, ministers, which it portrays in a linear and segmented way (Andrews, 2018; Shergold, 2015). This means how to manage this relationship in the design and development of reforms is open to being misunderstood by both ministers and public servants: ministers may mistakenly assume that because they have legitimate (hard) power in the system, they can simply promulgate a policy and order the Department to implement it, while departmental policy makers are sometimes of the equally misguided view that they alone are responsible for policy making and the only role of the minister is to take their advice. This case study indicates that both are required.

Theme 4: Staying close to schools

> Nothing beats visiting schools in order to understand schools. Talk to teachers, talk to principals and listen to what they say they need to improve their effectiveness.
>   If it doesn't work for schools, it doesn't work.
>
> Adrian Piccoli

The fourth theme drawn from the case study is the constant engagement by the Minister with principals and teachers.

As soon as he became the Opposition Education Spokesperson in 2009 and began developing the education election policy platform, Piccoli started visiting schools to learn what their key issues were. After he became Minister, it would have been easy to view himself as being at the top of the education system hierarchy, with schools and teachers at the bottom, and therefore only interacting with schools through the formal processes arranged by the Department. However, he quickly showed that he simply saw both schools and himself as different parts of a complex education system and believed he could and should interact directly with any part of it. There was rarely a week when he did not visit schools and meet with groups of principals from the local area, as well as occasionally dropping in on them unannounced.

He then used the knowledge he gained to have the Department change things that were not working well, or where the message they were getting from the education bureaucracy was not in accordance with the message he wanted to send, as well as to shape and refine policy development. He understood both the policy and political value of this, saying:

> It let me take the temperature of principals and teachers on areas we were considering reforming. I could road test ideas to see if they had support from the profession which sometimes ran contrary to the view of their industrial representatives or of the Department.

In addition to these meetings in schools, he also cultivated strong relationships with individual teachers. For example, at a Secondary Principals' Conference early in his tenure, a very well-regarded high school principal in Sydney, who was very sceptical of Ministers, asked him how he would know if the reforms were working. He said he didn't know but they were based on the best evidence available at the time and that only in time would principals and teachers be able to answer her question. About a year later, he called her with no warning. He reminded her of her question and asked her how she thought the answer was going. She was stunned that he recalled her question and she was surprised that he would take the time to seek her advice. She pointed out things that needed improving and he took her suggestions back to the Department to have them addressed. Then he called her every year after, on a random day, to ask her how the reforms were going. She became not only a great source of advice but one of his strongest advocates.

This is consistent with the limited research in this area which finds that teachers and principals are pivotal stakeholders in resisting and promoting reform; in the end, no meaningful education change can be achieved without their active cooperation so the most promising reform strategy is to establish direct lines of communication with them. Bruns and Schneider suggest that:

> Ministers and secretaries do well to maintain a schedule of continuous visits to schools, with no agenda other than to "listen" to teachers. This can generate feedback that genuinely improves the design and implementation of reforms, as well as build ground-level support for programs over time.
> *(2016, pp. 51–52)*

This is echoed by other former education ministers and secretaries. Wilson Risolia (2015), Secretary for Education in the State of Rio de Janiero, said that one of the greatest lessons was to "Be close to the schools" – visiting schools constantly and simply listening to feedback from teachers, directors and students. Similarly, former Australian Education Minister (later, Prime Minister) Julia Gillard said:

> Reflecting back on my time as Education Minister, what stands out is not the jousting with media or state ministers or the teachers' union. What comes to mind most vividly are my visits to schools. You could feel, touch, see the way our reforms were giving children a better chance in life.
> *(2014, n.p.)*

This theme is important because it highlights that the impacts of large-scale education system reform are primarily on schools: it is principals and teachers who have to make it work for their schools and their students and if it does not achieve that, it fails.

Theme 5: Using research evidence

> We had an ongoing commitment to evidence–based policy and we always had a published research base behind all our decisions.
>
> I constantly reminded my staff that "we don't make it up in the Minister's Office."
>
> Adrian Piccoli

The fifth theme relates to the use of evidence in the policy development process. The case study shows that at every stage of the development of LSLD, the Minister was intent on ensuring that the policy was based on evidence. As we saw in Theme 4, in particular, Piccoli listened to teachers and principals, saying:

> I spent a lot of time sitting on the floor in classrooms and sitting in staff rooms collecting "small data" about what teachers needed to improve their effectiveness.
>
> Experiencing and understanding the problem at the micro level is very powerful when arguing the case for reform to other leaders like Premiers and Treasurers as well as to the public.

The case study also demonstrated how the Minister interrogated the evidence which was collected by the Department and worked out how it could be used as part of the policy development process, as well as politically. This included the report of the consultation on LSLD, the evaluations of the *47 Schools Pilot* and the research the Department collected on school-based management.

There are some misconceptions that Ministers neither care about, nor read evidence. (In fact, one eminent professor of education told me dismissively that Ministers just got their junior political staff to summarise things for them but never read them.) However, that was certainly not the case with Minister Piccoli, who did not rely solely on what he was told by the Department. He also met regularly with policy experts and academics, with no Departmental staff present, to discuss their research and how he could incorporate their findings into the policies he was developing and would not hesitate to call them afterwards if he had questions. They included John Hattie, Pasi Sahlberg, David Hopkins, Brian Caldwell, Stephen Dinham and Michael Barber, all of whom gave valuable input to the policy development process.

The Minister also often asked questions about what the research showed about matters that had been raised by schools or by researchers and was frustrated when the Department had no answers or the capacity to provide them quickly. This led directly to his establishing the Centre for Education Statistics and Evaluation (CESE) within the Department in 2012. Its mandate was to undertake in-depth analyses of education practices and their effectiveness, using reliable data and knowledge, so that the evidence could then be used by himself and other policy makers to make more informed and better decisions about what to change and where to invest, as well as helping educators choose programs and strategies that actually work in their unique school settings.

At a meeting of Education Ministers from over 120 countries at the Education World Forum in London in 2014 he described his approach to the use of evidence in policy making, saying:

> We have recognised that systemic reform and improvement comes from the hard grind of data-based and evidence-backed policy work.
> (Piccoli, 2014, p. 2)

Shergold also argues that good policy depends on good advice which is factually accurate and backed by evidence. He contends that consultation should "harness knowledge from across government, other sectors and the public including the views of those likely to be impacted by the proposal" and that "advice should be informed by the latest thinking and practice from around the world while being alert to the Australian context" (2015, p. 17). This is consistent with research by Luetjens et al. which provides multiple case study examples from Australia and New Zealand of "successful public policies having their origins in conceptually coherent, evidence-informed advice" (2019, p. 17). It is also consistent with Shrestha et al.'s view that: "The principle of being structured yet flexible is to know that while systems should be driven by evidence, they are embedded in a broader political and economic context that is constantly in flux" (2019, p. 38).

This theme is significant as it shows the importance of evidence for politicians. It reveals how evidence underpinned the initial conceptualisation of the LSLD election promise, informed the Department's advice on the LSLD policy to the Minister and was also considered by the Minister in deciding on the policy parameters, thus providing a critical foundation on which the final LSLD policy document was grounded. This enabled the Minister to use all these sources of evidence politically as both a sword and a shield, to sell the LSLD policy to stakeholders and to deprive opponents of potential grounds for attack.

Theme 6: Power and policy making

> I carefully used my power to address the critical systemic education issues that matter whilst avoiding wasting our power on education irrelevancies. We were careful not to waste our political capital but nor were we afraid to spend it on good policy when we needed to.
>
> Adrian Piccoli

This theme relates to the importance of the use of power, by both Ministers and stakeholders, in the policy development process. Andrew Adonis, former UK Minister for Education, has commented: "Power is finite and evaporates much faster than you expect. It is vital to expend it on large, not small objects" (2012, p. 240), which is similar to Piccoli's view. However, there is only a small body of research literature in this area and it does not generally differentiate the range and types of political stakeholders, or explore the different strategies for dealing with them. For example, while Shrestha et al. (2019) document some strategies of political figures to leverage political capital and use soft power in Brazil, their case studies mainly report big-picture political trends and what "government" and "leaders" did or can do, rather than the processes used in managing the political context. The most comprehensive exploration of how the application of political power influences education policy making is provided by Carter and Piccoli (2024).

The LSLD case study provides insights into the ways in which the Minister used soft power – the ability to co-opt rather than coerce (Nye, 1990) – to manage the political context of the design of the policy including:

- Raising awareness of the reform through discourse with key stakeholders during the two years before the release of the LSLD election promise. This encouraged their engagement in its development and support for its direction.
- Ensuring that the LSLD narrative was being sold politically and that there was continued support for it by politicians and other NSW Government agencies such as Treasury. This was achieved by providing political material including speeches, articles and media releases for Government backbenchers to use in Parliament, in schools and with education stakeholders in their electorates, and also by regularly briefing the Treasurer and Premier.
- Using the announcement of LSLD to demonstrate to the community that the Government was delivering on its promises to devolve authority.

In addition to the power of the Minister to shape the policy development process, this theme also demonstrates how the political dynamics of education reform are influenced by the way in which the reform affects key stakeholders' interests, their relative power, and the effectiveness of their political strategies. This power of stakeholders is an area which is not well-researched. Teacher unions stand out as the education stakeholders with the most power as they generally have strong interests, wide geographic coverage, electoral impact and disruptive capacity (Bruns et al., 2019); however, much less attention has been given to other stakeholders who can play a pivotal role including teachers, principals and their associations, researchers and specialist policy makers.

The case study highlights that other groups and entities also have power to influence the reform development:

- In the early stages of discourse about large-scale system reform, while Piccoli was still the Opposition education spokesperson, the key education stakeholders had soft power to shape the reform by providing him with access to schools, as well as by letting him know what they would (and would not) support as part of the election policy.
- The Expenditure Review Committee of Cabinet had hard power in that it could have directed the Minister that LSLD was required to make budget savings, but he used his soft power to ensure that did not happen.
- The Department of Education financial policy makers had power over what was presented to the Minister as possible policy parameters, and that only ceased when the Minister used his hard power to direct that the reform was to be driven by educational rather than financial policy outcomes.
- The NSW Teachers Federation used its soft power of wide geographic coverage and potential electoral influence to try to prevent the LSLD policy from being developed, and then used its hard power of industrial action to try to stop its implementation.
- However, that also provides a good example of the importance of the power of stakeholders to influence policy more broadly through revealing how the development of LSLD was also caught up in a wider political power struggle between the NSWTF and the principals' associations over the possible formation of a Principals' Union. In that regard, the power and influence of the principals' associations in their support for LSLD, especially some of its more contentious elements, outweighed that of the union, and was critical in the NSWTF losing the battle to prevent the implementation of LSLD.

This theme is important as it demonstrates that the Minister had to use both his own hard and soft power to manage all these stakeholders differently. It also reveals that stakeholders too have power and that their relative power and their use of it was important in determining whether or not the reform could progress.

Theme 7: The relationship between policy and politics

> Get the balance between policy and politics right.
>
> Being an effective minister is 50% policy and 50% diplomacy. Too much diplomacy and you won't get anything done, too little diplomacy and you can't get anything done.
>
> Adrian Piccoli

A key theme drawn from the case study is the constant involvement of the Minister and his Office in both the development of the LSLD reform policy and, at the same time, in managing the political environment within which it was occurring. The case study indicates that they regarded policy and politics as two different but interrelated aspects of the same process, based on practical experience that: "Politics is what governments do. Policy is what they deliver" (Behm, 2015, p. 202). For example, only the Minister and his political staff could engage in the political aspects of managing stakeholders, whereas both they and the Departmental Liaison Officers could engage in consultations regarding the policy content of the reforms. (This is because under the Westminster system of government, DLOs are public servants on secondment to the Minister's Office and are not permitted to engage in political matters or give political advice to the Minister.) A further insight is that failure to understand the difference between policy and politics and to achieve an appropriate balance between them may result in failure to deliver the reform as both are required.

The literature on this issue is somewhat confused and contradictory. My research aligns with some conceptualisations of government public policy processes which acknowledge the roles of both ministers and public servants in policy development (e.g., Edwards et al., 2001) and also with memoirs by ministers (e.g., Adonis, 2012; Andrews, 2014; Gillard, 2014). On the other hand, it differs from recent research which generally sees the Departmental "public policy processes" as largely unrelated to the "political process" undertaken by the Minister, if indeed, it acknowledges the latter at all (e.g., Althaus et al., 2018; Ayres, 2021; Mercer et al., 2021; Washington & Mintrom, 2018). However, these views contradict the theoretical position taken in the education policy literature which posits that, as every policy emerges from some political process, politics and policy are not easily distinguished (Mitchell & Romero, 2018) and that any distinction between policy and politics is theoretically and empirically unsustainable (Gale, 2006).

With regard to the politics of education field, my case study differs from some research which considers only the political and institutional factors in explaining the development of education policies rather than the policies themselves, although it is consistent with Shrestha et al.'s contention that: "all technical inputs and political considerations must be coherent and aligned toward improved learning" (2019, p. 5).

Overall, the case study supports the argument that policy and politics are two sides of the same coin and the ministers must be involved simultaneously in both.

Theme 8: The Minister's leadership role in policy making

> As a Minister, developing large-scale, game-changing reform initiatives requires an appreciation of public policy, as well as leadership and political deftness.
> Adrian Piccoli

The final theme, which interweaves through the seven previous themes, is the leading and active role played by the Minister throughout the process of the reform development. As we have seen, this includes: articulating and developing the parameters of the initial policy for the devolution of authority while in Opposition; achieving and maintaining reform goal alignment around outcomes for principals and schools; defining the five core elements of the reform; continually engaging both formally and informally to achieve and maintain political and educational stakeholder support and manage opposition; and working with the Department to create the final form and content of the LSLD policy.

The Minister's leadership and decision-making at key points in the process were critical in setting and maintaining the direction of the reform and in determining the form and content of the final policy. However, it is noticeable that where the Minister and his staff were not fully engaged with the reform process, this correlated with little progress occurring and/or elements which might have resulted in a stronger policy not receiving sufficient attention. For example, for the first three months after the election, the Department executives were not receiving clear direction from the Minister on the goals of LSLD and therefore continued to progress their own managerialist efficiency and savings goal, until the Minister stepped in and explicitly rejected that approach. Similarly, while the Minister conceptualised the Five Fact Sheet form of the LSLD policy document, when its preparation was largely entrusted to the Department in February 2012, while he and his Office were involved in managing other contentious political issues, the final policy documents failed to include content regarding the expected outcomes of the reform and how implementation was to be managed. These are usual components of large-scale system reform documents (Shergold, 2015) and, in retrospect, the Minister and the key education stakeholders all consider their omission to be a significant failing in the LSLD policy.

The broad and continuous role taken by the Minister in the process of the development and design of LSLD aligns with Shrestha et al.'s (2019) finding that vision and leadership are major success factors in improving education systems and that elite commitment is necessary for quality reforms to occur. It is also consistent with recent descriptions of engagement and leadership by other former education ministers who report playing an active decision-making role throughout the reform conceptualisation and design process. For example, former Welsh Education Minister, Leighton Andrews, has said: "Ministers need to lead on policy. Prioritise a few core themes, develop and communicate your vision for the future" (2014, n.p.). Similarly, former UK Minister for Education Andrew Adonis, advises:

> Lead and explain, lead and explain. If you don't lead and explain, the public service machine stops, your party becomes restless, and opponents seize the momentum. You need to be a message-machine on constant 'replay'. And you need to be passionate and persuasive in what you believe, and convey this every day.
>
> *(2012, p. 245)*

However, this differs from the narrow and limited view taken in some of the more recent public policy literature, which either does not include politicians at all (e.g., Hartley et al., 2019; Moyson et al., 2017; Wu et al., 2015) or sees them as having only a limited role such as "support for the agency" (Mukherjee & Bali, 2019, p. 105) or "customers of policy advice" (Washington & Mintrom, 2018, p. 33). This raises the question as to whether these differing views of the role of governments and ministers, as expressed in the public policy literature and the politics of education literature, are sustainable; instead, it suggests that the leadership role of ministers needs to be recognised as a legitimate and necessary factor in the conceptualisation and development of large-scale education system reforms.

This issue is significant because it goes to the heart of the role of the minister in the process of developing large-scale education system reform: Is the minister the leader or not? And if they are, what is their role? This case study, as well as the accounts of former ministers, would indicate the answer to that question is in the affirmative.

Bringing the themes together: politics, policy, processes and people

These eight key cross-cutting themes which thread through and across the case study enable us to better understand the roles of the actors, politics and what parts of the political processes of this large-scale system reform went well or poorly, which are "still largely a 'black box'" (Busemeyer & Trampusch, 2011, p. 432). When considered in conjunction with the detailed Analytical Reflections in the four chapters of the case study, they particularly assist us to better appreciate the complex, multi-faceted and over-arching role of politicians as policy makers in the development of large-scale system reform.

Taken together, the themes demonstrate that developing education policy cannot be separated from politics and reveal the relationships between politics, power and policy. They highlight the importance of the Minister's leadership in establishing the strategic reform direction and determining the final policy and also elucidate the uses made of research evidence. They illuminate the value of his strong relationships and continual engagement with a wide range of stakeholders, including school leaders, throughout the process, together with the complex "policy dance" that occurs between the Minister and the Department.

While this gives important insights into the policy development process itself, all those engaged in whole system reform still require practical strategic frameworks and guiding principles that they can actually use in developing education policies to achieve overall system transformation. That is the focus of the final chapter.

8
STRATEGIC FRAMEWORKS AND GUIDING PRINCIPLES FOR WHOLE SYSTEM IMPROVEMENT

> There is no silver bullet, no glib one-liner, for ensuring success for all students in school education. Genuine, sustained improvement comes from data-based, evidence-backed systemic and classroom practice reform, wide consultation with stakeholders and, as a result, not being afraid to try new things.
>
> (Adrian Piccoli)

While there have been many attempts to construct theory-informed explanations of real-world public policy making practices (Mercer et al., 2021), the politics of education continue to be under-researched, under-analysed and under-theorised (Andrews, 2017, 2018; Bruns & Schneider, 2016; Gift & Wibbels, 2014; Hartley, 2010; Moe, 2012; Shrestha et al., 2019). As a result, there still exists considerable debate and critique about the purposes, approaches and outcomes of policy approaches to transforming education systems within and across countries (Campbell, 2017). In particular, there do not appear to be any practical models or frameworks which provide clear guidance for politicians, policy makers, educational leaders and researchers regarding the process of conceptualising, developing and initiating large-scale education system reform. Also, differing views about what makes reforms work, and also why they fail, mean that the applicability and generalisability of the research from one context to another remains problematic. Indeed, Hopkins et al. (2014, p. 272) caution that there is no "reform in a box" that can be simply brought in and implemented.

Nonetheless, the continuing research and interest in this area demonstrate its importance and I know from experience that ministers, stakeholders and policy makers would all benefit from guidance on how to go about developing large-scale education system reforms, even if there is no "recipe" for it. So, while the case study provides important new knowledge about the role of politicians as policy makers, the problem remains that there is no agreed framework for the education policy development process to achieve success in large-scale education system reform or that assists all those who are involved in it. Spillane argues that this is necessary because:

> Diagnosis [figuring out what is going on, defining goals and identifying strategies to ameliorate identified problems] and design [shaping aspects of the situation in purposeful ways to address particular goals] require a conceptual or analytical framework to guide and focus the work... Absent such frameworks, practitioners, policymakers and researchers are simply talking past one another.
>
> *(2013, p. 39)*

It would therefore be helpful to have some practical strategic frameworks that are relevant and useful to all those engaged in developing large-scale education system reform in a range of contexts and jurisdictions.

I therefore reflected on the existing public policy and education policy theories to make further sense of the eight themes drawn from the practical policy making experiences of the *Local Schools, Local Decisions* (LSLD) case study. Based on these reflections, I have developed three frameworks which connect theory with practice and which go to different aspects of policy development. My aim in creating them is to synthesise a number of aspects of large-scale education system reform development and map them in a way which is conceptually relevant, systematic and practically actionable for politicians, practitioners, policy makers and researchers in the policy development process[1].

Framework 1: The "Policy Process Bow Tie"

My first framework builds on Stephen Ball's theory of policy as both text and discourse (1990, 1993, 1994a). Ball theorised a policy-cycle approach which emphasises the contexts of influence, text production and practice. It rejects a linear, two-dimensional, top-down educational management concept of policy/implementation relationships and instead recognises the "discontinuities, compromises, omissions and exceptions" inherent in policy and in its production (Ball, 1990, p. 3). In the case study analysis, we have seen how this concept is helpful in explaining aspects of the development of the LSLD policy as it moved between "policy as discourse" and "policy as text" at each stage of the cycle. However, while Ball's theory is helpful in understanding the concept of policy being both text and discourse, it does not provide any guidance to politicians as to how they might apply it in practice.

Reflecting on this led me to link it to former Welsh Education Minister Leighton Andrews' (2017) notion of the cycle of policy development as it applies to ministers.

He suggests this could involve: the shaping of an initial policy idea; the process of manifesto preparation and adoption; consultation; policy instructions to government lawyers; and, if required, the preparation of legislation. This "politician's view" is different from the policy cycle frameworks that relate to the public sector's role in policy development, such as Althaus et al.'s (2018) Australian Policy Cycle. Finally, I reflected on how these two ideas – Ball's based in theory and Andrews' based in practice – might link to the case study, to create a framework which brings them all together.

The case study showed how shaping the initial policy idea of LSLD began with Piccoli's discourse with stakeholders while in Opposition, then moved to the production of the first "text" – the election policy. After the election, there was further discourse around the goals and detailed purpose of the policy, which again led to the production of "text" – the Minister's statement of the five areas and eleven directions of LSLD and the Department's LSLD Discussion Paper. This was followed by the consultation and engagement discourse with stakeholders and finally the production of the Five Fact Sheets as the LSLD policy text which was announced by the Minister. This then led to further discourse around implementation and the creation of further text of the policy in practice (although this final stage is beyond the scope of this book which extends only to the announcement of the LSLD policy and not to its implementation).

In summary, the case study shows that LSLD was developed through a process of wide-ranging messy, complex discourse which led to minimal statements of text, which then led to more discourse and so on. At each stage, each iteration of the text provided a common framework and parameters within which the next stage of the discourse took place and thereby ensured that practitioners and policy makers were not "simply talking past one another" (Spillane, 2013, p. 39). This policy process can be depicted in the framework shown in Figure 8.1.

This framework shows how discourse and text are ongoing in a continuous *Policy Process Bow Tie*. Discourse is deliberately depicted as being a much larger component of the process than text, which was in fact the case in the development of LSLD; and the process is also shown as being open at both ends of the framework, which reflects that it has no definitive starting or end points. In between each of the discourse elements, the text provides clear way-points which frame, structure and connect the next part of the discourse. This new framework provides a good explanation of the policy process used in developing LSLD.

However, as Kurt Lewin famously noted, "nothing is so practical as a good theory" (1943, p. 336), so I also reflected on the lessons from the case study and how this framework may have assisted us practically if it had been available to the Minister's Office before we started on the reform journey. I considered how it might be useful to politicians, practitioners, policy makers and researchers more

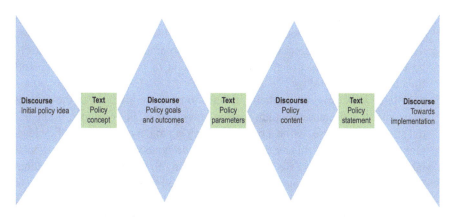

FIGURE 8.1 The Policy Process Bow Tie Framework
Source: Dudley (2023, p. 182).

widely in the development of large-scale education system reform. Six features stand out.

1 The framework provides a dynamic model of the process rather than a static depiction. This reflects the reality of what occurs during policy development. This gives guidance to all those involved as to the issues on which to focus at each stage of the discourse, as well as the potential content of each iteration of the text production.
2 The framework shows the importance of discourse in the process, both in its scale, as well as how it builds on and further develops the policy text. This underscores the importance and value of engagement between all actors in the education policy making system at every stage of the process, rather than simply though a single, formal consultation mechanism as depicted in most policy cycle frameworks.
3 As the case study shows, we did not appreciate, nor pay sufficient attention to, the role of discourse in achieving the alignment of goals and identifying the intended outcomes of the reforms. The Minister was reactive during the early part of the process, rather than proactively leading and framing the discourse, and this may have played a part in the lengthy delays in moving the development of the policy forward over the first four months. The *Policy Process Bow Tie* framework would have given guidance to our process and may have resulted in less delay in aligning the goals, as well as a clear outcome statement for the reform.
4 When the Department was drafting the LSLD Five Fact Sheets policy document, we did not have a clear appreciation that the manner in which the policy implementation process would be directed and oversighted would be the critical to the long-term future of the reform and to which, as the

Minister and the educational leaders identified, we failed to give sufficient attention. The open-ended discourse box in the framework may have alerted us to the need for clearer statements about implementation and outcomes to be included in the text of the policy document to frame the next stages of the discourse.

5 The framework provides explicit guidance to all those involved in the process as to what the discourse should focus on at each stage. For example, in the initial stage of discourse, while a politician is trying to develop a new policy idea, practitioners can use this as the opportunity to advocate for where particular large-scale system reform is needed by providing first-hand information about what is actually happening in schools through both meetings and invitations to visit. It is also an opportunity for researchers and policy advocates to provide evidence of what has worked successfully in other jurisdictions and suggest how that could be applied in a new policy.

At the later stage of discourse around the policy content, its focus moves to the specific reforms to be contained in the final policy document. Here the politicians and policy makers can test policy proposals with practitioners to see if it could actually be implemented in schools, what opposition might be expected, what changes to other policies might be needed, whether there is the capacity in the system to make it happen and what resources would be required to support it. There is also the opportunity for further engagement between policy makers and researchers regarding what evidence is available to support the specific proposals.

6 The framework calls out the common, but misguided, idea that policy statements appear fully formed and complete in their first iteration. This is very rarely the case. In fact, as the framework shows they evolve from a broad idea, through increasingly definitive statements of the policy parameters, to the final text, through a process of drafting and refinement, which is informed through discourse. An understanding of this supports and relieves pressure on policy makers by giving them permission (and perhaps, encouragement) to produce policy drafts during the process. It also assures practitioners, researchers and policy advocates that the early policy iterations are not final so they do not feel shut out or discouraged from continuing to participate in the policy development process just because there is an initial policy text.

These examples show that the *Policy Process Bow Tie* is a simple practical framework which can give guidance to all those involved in the policy development of large-scale education system reforms as to what the discourse should concentrate on at each stage of the process and what the focus of the policy text production output should be.

It relates strongly to three of the themes identified in the previous chapter: the engagement with key education stakeholders (Theme 2), the Minister's relationship with the Department (Theme 3) and using evidence (Theme 5). These are all features of the research on education policy.

However, it does not directly capture the themes which relate to the political aspects of policy making, which are a focus of the politics of education research. These are the importance of the political context (Theme 1), power and policy making (Theme 6), the relationship between policy and politics (Theme 7) and the Minister's leadership in policy making (Theme 8). In particular, the *Policy Process Bow Tie* does not portray the dynamics of the interaction between the stakeholders during the process. Nor does it recognise "the paramount importance of politics in determining whether policy progresses from stage to stage and at what pace" (Edwards et al., 2001, p. 184) and that, sooner or later, each stage of the policy discourse is cut off by political decisions as politicians exercise leadership by stepping in and taking responsibility for the policy decisions, which results in the next iteration of the policy text.

Further frameworks are therefore required to capture other aspects of the process.

Framework 2: The Education Policy and Engagement System

As I was reflecting on the practical and theoretical utility of the *Policy Process Bow Tie*, it occurred to me that if it were given to ministers and their staff, or to policy makers, researchers and practitioners more generally, the next question would likely be: "Well if that's the process, who do I talk to, what do I talk to them about, and how does that get turned into policy decisions and policy documents?"

In the Minister's Office, we did not have a clear answer to this question and from my own previous experience both as a stakeholder and a departmental policy maker I know that often others involved in the process do not either. This led me to consider that a second framework might be useful and to ponder on whether there were any theories which, combined with insights from the case study, the eight themes and the *Policy Process Bow Tie*, might assist in devising one.

In the case study, and in relation to Ball's theory of policy as text and discourse, we saw that developing the LSLD reform policy was not a linear, formal process aligned with the legitimate hierarchical authority system structure with the Minister at the top of the pyramid and the teachers far off at the bottom of it (both in actual and power differential terms). Rather, it was messy, interconnected and multi-dimensional, and involved many system actors with different interests and connections, which can be explained by complex systems theory (Lemke & Sabelli, 2008). However, as I reflected on the themes, it was apparent that the complex education system as generally portrayed (e.g., by Goldspink, 2007) is static and high-level and does not fully capture the complexity of the system within which a minister operates. Nor does it provide guidance as to the minister's role and relationships with other actors in it during the policy development process.

To develop a framework which provides such guidance, I drew on complex systems theory to locate the policy making components, and more specifically, politicians and their education departments, within the broader education system, and within the political system. I then linked this with Bruns et al.'s (2019) intensive and extensive identification and examination of education reform stakeholders, and the categorisation of them as insiders or outsiders, which they believe could have value for reformers who lack either prior experience in government and politics, or in education. Finally, I considered how the key issues arising from the eight themes could be incorporated and through these two ideas, one theoretical and the other drawn from politics of education case studies, I synthesised and mapped a dynamic, fine-grained education system engagement framework to provide guidance to ministers and other education system actors in the policy development process for large-scale education system reform. This is shown in Figure 8.2.

This framework elegantly captures the key elements that arise from five of the eight key themes in the LSLD case study. It shows the relationship, engagement and decision-making processes between the Minister and his Office and the Education Department, which are at the heart of education system reform policy development (Theme 3). It identifies the range of key stakeholders and actors

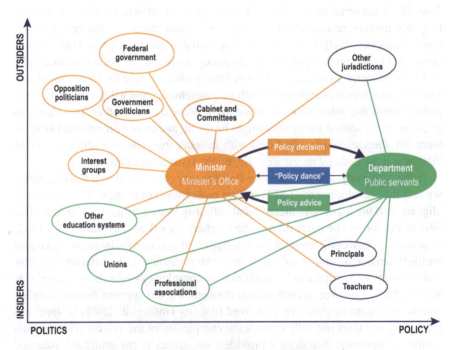

FIGURE 8.2 Education Policy and Engagement System Framework

Source: Dudley (2023, p. 185).

Strategic Frameworks and Guiding Principles **129**

and locates them towards either the political or the policy end of the spectrum and portrays whether they are more insiders or outsiders in the education context (Theme 2). It differentiates between the consultation and engagement undertaken by the Department (shown in green) which is generally with insiders (in the bottom half of the framework) and always focused on policy, and that undertaken by the Minister (shown in orange), which is with both insiders and outsiders and includes the political context (the top left quadrant) (Theme 1), as well as policy considerations (Theme 7). Finally, and most importantly, it locates the Minister in the centre of the system (Theme 8). This clearly recognises their essential role as the leader in large-scale education system reform development, positioned at the intersections of policy with politics and of insiders with outsiders.

This Framework provides guidance as to the variety of stakeholders who should be engaged in the discourse by the Minister and the Department, whether this discourse has a focus on politics or policy, and how public servants work with the Minister through the "policy dance" to develop policy as text. It would therefore be very helpful for policy actors in education policy development, especially when used in conjunction with the *Policy Process Bow Tie*. However, it does not directly capture three other key themes: staying close to schools (Theme 4), using evidence (Theme 5) and power and policy making (Theme 6).

This means that while both these frameworks are helpful in their own right, neither of them encompasses all of the themes that can be seen in the education policy development process nor do they capture the theme of power and policy making at all. An additional framework is therefore required to put it all together.

Framework 3: Whole System Reform Policy Development

The eight themes drawn from the case study of LSLD demonstrate that developing policy for whole system improvement cannot be separated from politics. They highlight that the Minister's leadership is a core element, together with the importance of consultation and engagement with stakeholders throughout the process, as well as the "policy dance" that occurs between the Department and the Minister. They show that education system reform and policy making are not straightforward and that content and process also cannot be separated. Rather, they are "diverse, dynamic, disorderly in process, embedded in their political context, and have complexity and many policy actors involved" who must incorporate the contextual factors of "policy, politics, and people (the three Ps)" into the process (Pont, 2018, pp. 182–183).

When viewed from that perspective, the eight themes fall into three groups:

1 The *parameters of policy development*.
   - The *political context* and its impact on policy development (Themes 1 and 7). This includes politicians as well as Treasury and the Cabinet. This parameter

determines what reform policies are possible and not possible because of the historical and political context as well as political ideologies. It includes considerations of their feasibility and the capacity of the system to implement them, both financially and practically, and their alignment with other government policies and priorities.
- *Power and policy making* (Theme 6). This relates to the hard and soft power of the Minister to influence both the policy making process and support for the changes, as well as to make decisions when required. It also includes the hard and soft power of stakeholders to support or oppose reforms.
- *Research evidence* (Theme 5). This includes the research evidence on whole system reform about what works and what does not work for school improvement, evidence on policy and practice, as well as on current issues impacting the education system. This is the domain of the researchers who develop the evidence which underpins informed policy decisions.

2 The *policy actors*.
- The *Minister* for Education who leads the reform development (Theme 8). This includes both political and policy staff in the Minister's Office.
- The *Education Authority* (Theme 3). This is the government authority responsible for the education system, which is overseen by the Minister and which will be required to implement the policy.
- The *key education stakeholders* (Theme 2). This includes teacher unions and principals' associations.

3 Those on whom whole system policy improvement will have the greatest *impacts* (Theme 4). This is the schools, including the principals, teachers and students.

I then positioned the elements of each of these three groups in a new overarching heuristic framework which shows the relationships between them and which includes all the dimensions of whole system policy making which have been identified in this analysis. This is shown in Figure 8.3.

This framework encompasses all of the eight themes regarding the three key policy actors, the three key policy parameters and the policy impacts. In particular, it reveals how the six elements of policy making, shown in the six points of the star, are the critical inputs into the development of whole system school improvement policy.

It captures the dimensions of policy, politics and power by indicating that during the policy making process, the Minister interacts with the stakeholders through a power parameter. As the case study revealed, the Minister used soft power during the discourse phases of the *Policy Process Bow Tie* to persuade other policy actors and gain support for the policy parameters. He then used the hard power of decision-making in relation to determining the policy text at the conclusion of each discourse phase, thereby setting the new parameters for the next discourse stage of the process.

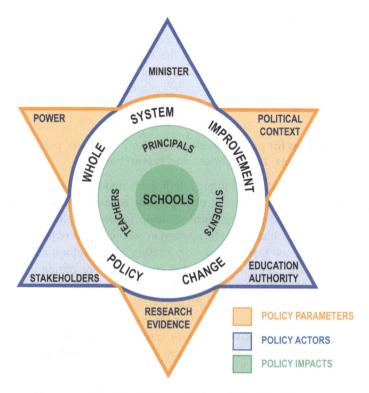

FIGURE 8.3 Framework for Whole System Reform Policy Development

The Framework also reveals how the Minister and the Minister's Office staff engage with the senior executives and policy makers in the Education Authority within a political and historical context. This effectively determines the boundaries of what can and cannot be included in the policy. When this context is ignored, or not recognised, policy development is likely to stall or fail, as we saw in the early stages of the development of LSLD, when the Department (the Education Authority in NSW) did not take into account the policy and political positioning of the new government and the Minister was slow to make this clear.

The Framework demonstrates that informed policy rests on a base of research evidence and how that evidence feeds into policy development by both the Education Authority and the stakeholders and then, through them, to the Minister, who is appropriately located in the leadership position at the top of the Framework. Most importantly, it highlights that any policy changes will impact most on schools – the principals, the teachers and the students – which are at the centre of the process and which must therefore always be at the forefront of policy development considerations.

This new *Framework for Whole System Education Policy Development* provides an overarching heuristic that encompasses the key policy actors, the policy parameters and the policy impacts and shows the relationships between them and, in many ways, it provides the policy development framework precursor to the OECD's *Implementing Education Policies Framework* (2020). Together with the *Policy Process Bow Tie Framework* and the *Education Policy and Engagement System Framework*, it can guide and focus the process of education policy development by enabling policy actors to understand how all elements of the policy development system relate and interact.

Guiding principles for policy development for politicians, policy makers, stakeholders, practitioners and researchers

My aim in writing this book is to provide insights into the role of politicians as policy makers in the development of large-scale education system reform and to distil lessons and identify practical strategic frameworks for whole system improvement reform which might be relevant in other contexts or jurisdictions.

At the start, we saw that large-scale education system reform is a key focus for governments around the world but that few of them are getting it right. And that, while politicians are key players in whole system improvement, what stands out is that there are no generally agreed theoretical models or frameworks which provide clear guidance for them regarding the process of conceptualising, developing and initiating large-scale education system reform. There is no "reform in a box" that can be simply brought in and implemented (Hopkins et al., 2014, p. 272).

Nonetheless, I knew from my experience that those engaged in developing large-scale education system reform require guidance on how to go about it, and that, even if there is no "recipe" for it, some clear practical advice, based on research, would be helpful. I therefore reflected on the insights regarding the role of politicians as policy makers drawn from the case study, the eight themes, and my three new practical strategic frameworks. I then used inductive analysis to draw all these together and synthesise them into guiding principles for politicians, policy makers, stakeholders, practitioners and researchers. There were many of these, so I used reflective thematic analysis to develop patterns in the long list, and I drew on my experience as a Chief of Staff to conceptualise what lessons would be most useful.

My challenge was then how to present the resulting short list. My first option was to use the more formal, generalised language of academic research findings. However, I was mindful of Mercer et al.'s concern that "practitioners do not see academic insights as directly useful to their policy activities" (2021, p. 4), and it seemed that it would be more useful to frame them in a way that might be more practical and relevant for those who might use them. To do so, I recalled my insider positionality as a Chief of Staff and I imagined briefing a new Minister and Minister's Office staff, as well as the Department and key stakeholders, about what it would be helpful for them to bear in mind in working collaboratively together to develop effective policy for whole system reform.

From these reflections, I developed the following *Ten Guiding Principles*, which are short, clear, practical, and designed to speak directly to politicians, policy makers, stakeholders, practitioners and researchers.

GUIDING PRINCIPLES FOR POLITICIANS, POLICY MAKERS, STAKEHOLDERS, PRACTITIONERS AND RESEARCHERS DEVELOPING WHOLE SYSTEM REFORM POLICY

1 *Whole system reform requires politicians to have a clear vision of change and to provide the leadership to drive it.* The Minister's role is to lead on both the policy and politics through every step of the reform development process, from the first idea through to its announcement and implementation.
2 *Always focus on the best interests of schools and students* and be clear about what outcomes you want to achieve for them from the reform. If it doesn't work for schools, it doesn't work, so don't do it.
3 *Be sensitive to the historical and political context.* All reform decisions are situated in a context defined by government commitments and political ideology, a history of prior policies and a budgetary framework.
4 *Effective policy development requires engaged and purposeful dialogue and collaboration between all policy actors in the education and wider political systems.* This includes politicians, public servants, practitioners, policy makers and researchers as well as teachers, principals and key education stakeholders. Tailor the engagement and consultation strategy with each, and also the use of soft and hard power, to balance or use with or against each other.
5 *Understand what stage the policy development process of discourse about the policy, and production of the policy text is up to.* Align your engagement strategy to respond to the focus of the discourse at that stage.
6 *Trust the profession and consult widely.* Take the profession with you in a positive, inclusive and constructive way.
7 *Listen, engage and learn before you act.* Ensure all views are considered and all advice tested with everyone – the Minister, the Department, the key stakeholders, the principals, the schools and the political players.
8 *Ensure the policy rests on a solid base of research evidence.* Use it to inform the design of the policy and to build support and counter opposition.
9 *Establish a collaborative, open and positive relationship between the Minister, the Minister's Office and the Department.* Ensure there are clearly agreed understandings, directions and expectations for the reform and that all the goals are aligned.
10 *Stay on top of reform development and implementation, and preferably in front of it.* Ensure the execution of the policy, the monitoring of its implementation and the evaluation of the outcomes are built into the reform design.

Concluding Reflection: Why it matters for whole system school improvement

Despite the increasing role of governments in large-scale school system reform, the difficulty in achieving it and general agreement that politicians are integral to it, there is little clear guidance they might use in conceptualising, developing and initiating whole system school improvement in the political contexts within which they operate. There are no firm right answers, no agreed processes or frameworks for undertaking it and no "reform in a box" solution they can easily apply. Ministers are therefore faced with a series of dilemmas and decisions as they develop education policy without such knowledge they can use to guide them.

However, this is not only a problem for the politicians: it also makes it difficult for all the other participants in the education policy making process – practitioners, policy makers, stakeholders and researchers as well as schools – to engage fully and effectively with politicians and make it more likely that reforms that deliver whole system school improvement will be developed and implemented.

It is my hope that this book will improve education policy making and thereby enhance education system reform in five ways.

Firstly, the new knowledge it provides on the *role of politicians in developing education policy for system reform* gives insights into what actually happens in a Minister's Office, while the eight themes delineate the key matters of which Ministers must be cognisant in the reform process. This should assist them to better understand their role and the issues involved and therefore to more effectively lead the development of policy for reform.

Secondly, the *Policy Process Bow Tie Framework* enhances collaboration between politicians, practitioners, policy makers and researchers in improving education systems by enabling them to determine what stage of discourse or text the policy development process is up to at any time. They can then tailor their engagement strategies to be most effective at each stage of the reform process.

Thirdly, the *Education Policy and Engagement System Framework* enhances engaged and purposeful dialogue between politicians, policy makers, practitioners and wider school communities, though enabling an understanding of the wider system within which education policy development takes place. It identifies the key players who should be engaged in the discourse with the Minister and the Department – both insiders and outsiders – and whether this has a focus on politics or policy. It also shows how public servants work with the Minister through the "policy dance" for advice to be given and decisions made on policy.

Fourthly, and of vital importance, the *Framework for Whole System Reform Policy Development* provides an overarching heuristic that depicts for the first time the key policy actors, policy parameters and policy impacts. It demonstrates how all those participating in the process are connected and related, thereby providing them with new ways of understanding and engaging in the development of large-scale system reform policy.

Finally, the *Ten Guiding Principles* for developing whole system education reform policy provide key takeouts which all those involved in the policy development process should all keep in mind and use as the basis for their decision-making and actions.

It is my hope that these insights, practical frameworks and guiding principles can together shape and focus the process of education policy development, so that politicians, practitioners, policy makers, key stakeholders and researchers are able to talk with, rather than past one another and collaboratively design effective policies for whole system school improvement.

Note

1 I am using Mercer et al.'s (2021) definition of the term "framework" here as it connotes a looser construct of ideas and concepts than a model and seeks to help understanding and guide action, without claiming unerring predictive power or perfect utility in all circumstances.

APPENDIX
Local Schools, Local Decisions: Fact Sheets

This set of five *Local Schools, Local Decisions Fact Sheets* was released by the NSW Minister for Education on 11 March 2012.

Source: This material has been adapted/remixed/transformed/built upon from "Local Schools, Local Decisions: Fact Sheets". © State of New South Wales (Department of Education) (unless indicated otherwise), 2023, licensed under a CC (Creative Commons) BY 4.0.

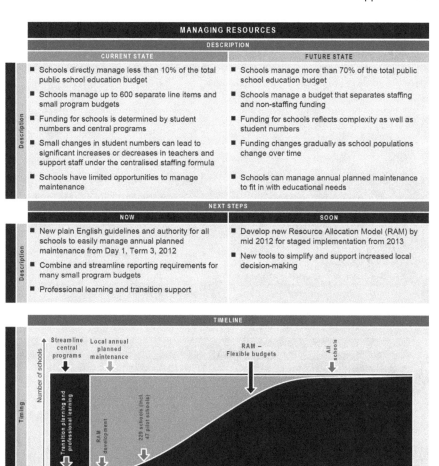

FIGURE A.1 Local Schools, Local Decisions Fact Sheet: Managing Resources

138 Appendix

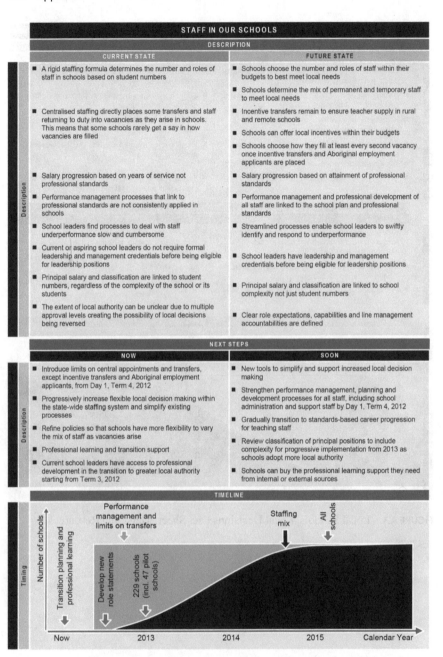

FIGURE A.2 Local Schools, Local Decisions Fact Sheet: Staff in our Schools

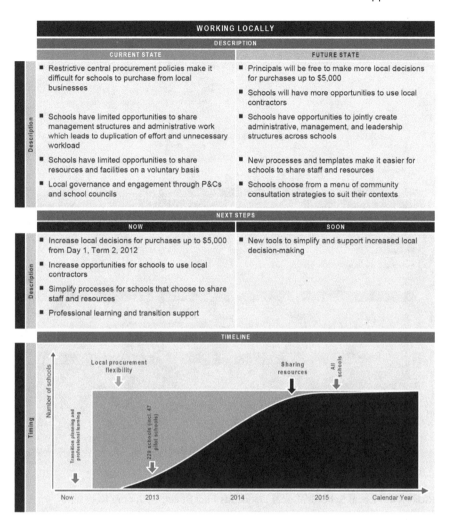

FIGURE A.3 Local Schools, Local Decisions Fact Sheet: Working Locally

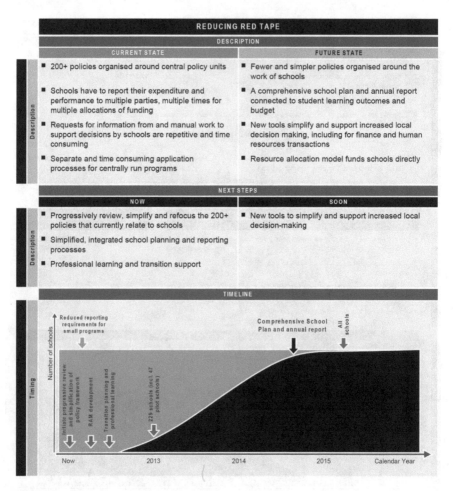

FIGURE A.4   Local Schools, Local Decisions Fact Sheet: Reducing Red Tape

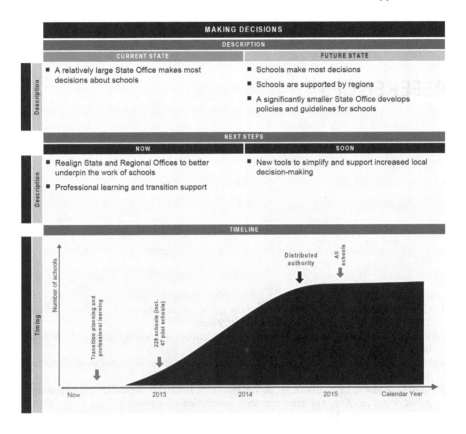

FIGURE A.5 Local Schools, Local Decisions Fact Sheet: Making Decisions

REFERENCES

ABC News. (2012, June 27). *NSW teachers go on strike*. https://www.abc.net.au/news/2012-06-27/nsw-teachers-to-go-on-strike/4094666

Adonis, A. (2012). *Education, education, education: Reforming England's schools*. Biteback Publishing Ltd.

Althaus, C., Bridgman, P., & Davis, G. (2018). *The Australian policy handbook: A practical guide to the policy making process* (6th ed.). Allen & Unwin.

Althaus, C., Carson, L., Sullivan, H., & van Wanrooy, B. (2021). Research and education in public sector practice: a systems approach to understanding policy impact. *Policy Design and Practice*, *4*(3), 309–322. https://doi.org/10.1080/25741292.2021.1977478

Andrews, L. (2014). *Ministering to education: A reformer reports*. Parthian Books (e-book).

Andrews, L (2017). How can we demonstrate the public value of evidence-based policy making when government ministers declare that the people 'have had enough of experts'? *Palgrave Communications*, *3*(1), 1–9.

Andrews, L. (2018). Telling governance stories: From lecturer, to minister, and back! *PS, Political Science and Politics*, *51*(1), 165–168. https://doi.org/10.1017/S1049096517001871

Angus, M. (2005). *The rules of school reform*. Taylor & Francis e-library.

ARTD Consultants. (2011). *Independent review of the school based management pilot: Final report*. ARTD Pty Ltd.

Australian Politics (2001, October 23). *Liberals attack Beazley over Knowledge Nation* [Press release]. https://australianpolitics.com/2001/10/23/liberals-attack-beazley-over-knowledge-nation.html

Ayres, R. (2021). Using the policy cycle: Practice into theory and back again. In T. Mercer, R. Ayres, B. Head, & J. Wanna (Eds.), *Learning policy, doing policy: Interactions between public policy theory, practice and teaching* (pp. 185–204). ANU Press.

Baker, K. (1993). *The turbulent years: My life in politics*. Faber and Faber.

Baker, L. K. (2015). The revolution begins. In R. Pring & M. Roberts (Eds.), *A generation of radical educational change: Stories from the field* (pp. 19–25). Routledge.

Ball, S. (1990). *Politics and policy making in education: Explorations in policy sociology*. Routledge.

Ball, S. J. (1993). What is policy? Texts, trajectories and toolboxes. *The Australian Journal of Education Studies*, *13*(2), 10–17. https://doi.org/10.1080/0159630930130203

Ball, S. J. (1994a). *Education reform: A critical and post structural approach*. Open University Press.
Ball, S. J. (1994b). Researching inside the state: Issues in the interpretation of elite interviews. In D. Halpin & B. Troyna (Eds.), *Researching education policy: Ethical and methodological issues* (pp. 107–120). Falmer Press.
Ball, S. J (2015). What is policy? 21 years later: Reflections on the possibilities of policy research. *Discourse Studies in the Cultural Politics of Education, 36*(3), 306–313.
Ball, S. J., Braun, A., & Maguire, M. (2012). *How schools do policy: Policy enactment in secondary schools*. Routledge.
Barber, M. (2015). *How to run a government so that citizens benefit and taxpayers don't go crazy*. Allen Lane.
Barber, M., & Fullan, M (2005). Tri-level development: It's the system. *Education Week, 24*(25), 32–35.
Barber, M., & Mourshed, M. (2007). *How the world's best performing systems came out on top*. McKinsey & Co.
Barker, G. (2006, October 14). The story Barry Jones won't tell. *Australian Financial Review*. https://www.afr.com/politics/the-story-barry-jones-wont-tell-20061014-j7020
Beder, S. (2008, November 26). Big business dominates educational planning. *Sydney Morning Herald*. https://www.smh.com.au/national/big-business-dominates-educational-planning-20081126-gdt49j.html
Behm, A. (2015). *No, minister: So you want to be a chief of staff?* Melbourne University Publishing.
Birkland, T. A. (2016). *An introduction to the policy process: Theories, concepts, and models of public policy making* (4th ed.). Routledge.
Blunkett, D. (2006). *The Blunkett tapes: My life in the bear pit*. Bloomsbury Publishing.
Boutgatsas, T (2011). Piccoli addresses equity conference. *Education, 92*(9), 11.
Braun, V., & Clarke, V. (2006). Using thematic analysis in psychology. *Qualitative Research in Psychology, 3*(2), 77–101. https://doi:10.1191/1478088706qp063oa
Braun, V., & Clarke, V. (2013). *Successful qualitative research: A practical guide for beginners*. Sage.
Breakspear, S. (2012). The policy impact of PISA: An exploration of the normative effects of international benchmarking in school system performance. In *OECD Education Working Papers*, No. 71. OECD Publishing. https://doi.org/10.1787/5k9fdfqffr28-en
Breakspear, S. (2014). *How does PISA shape education policy making? Why how we measure learning determines what counts in education. Seminar Series 240*. Centre for Strategic Education.
Bridgman, P., & Davis, G. (2000). *The Australian policy handbook* (first published in 1998). Allen & Unwin.
Bruns, B., & Luque, J. (2015). *Great teachers: How to raise student learning in Latin America and the Caribbean*. World Bank Publications.
Bruns, B., Macdonald, I. H., & Schneider, B. R. (2019). The politics of quality reforms and the challenges for SDGs in education. *World Development, 118*, 27–38. https://doi.org/10.1016/j.worlddev.2019.02.008
Bruns, B., & Schneider, B. R. (2016). Managing the politics of quality reforms in education: Policy lessons from global experience. Background paper for report: *The learning generation: Investing in education for a changing world*. International Commission on Financing Global Education Opportunity.
Busemeyer, M., & Trampusch, C (2011). Comparative political science and the study of education. *British Journal of Political Science, 41*(2), 413–443.
Caldwell, B. (2007). *Principal autonomy research project*. Retrieved from Educational Transformations website: http://educationaltransformations.com.au/wp-content/uploads/Principal+Autonomy+Final+Report.pdf

Caldwell, B. J. (1997). The future of public education: A policy framework for lasting reform. *Educational Management and Administration. BELMAS, 25*(4), 357–370.
Caldwell, B. J. (2016). Impact of school autonomy on student achievement: Cases from Australia. *International Journal of Educational Management, 30*(7), 1171–1187. https://doi.org/10.1108/IJEM-10-2015-0144
Caldwell, B. J., & Hayward, D. K. (1998). *The future of schools: Lessons from the reform of public education*. The Falmer Press.
Campbell, C. (2015). Leading system-wide educational improvement in Ontario. In A. Harris & M. Jones (Eds.), *Leading futures: Global perspectives on educational leadership* (pp. 71–78). Sage.
Campbell, C (2017). Developing teachers' professional learning. *Canadian Journal of Education, 40*(2), 1–33.
Carr, K (2009). Coalition plan to lift 'bottom 25 per cent. *Education, 90*(7), 3.
Carr, K (2011). Faces change at education helm. *Education, 92*(4), 5.
Carter, D., & Piccoli, A. (2024). *Power, politics, and the playground: Perspectives on power and authority in education*. Routledge.
Centre for Education Statistics and Evaluation. (2018). *Local schools, local decisions: Evaluation interim report*. NSW Department of Education. cese.nsw.gov.au
Centre for Education Statistics and Evaluation. (2020). *Local schools, local decisions: Evaluation final report*. NSW Department of Education. cese.nsw.gov.au
Chapman, C., & Fullan, M. (2007). Collaboration and partnership for equitable improvement: Towards a networked learning system? *School Leadership & Management, 27*(3), 207–211. https://doi.org/10.1080/13632430701379354
Cohen, D. K (1995). What is the system in systemic reform? *Educational Researcher, 24*(9), 11–17.
Cohen, L., Manion, L., & Morrison, K. (2017). *Research methods in education* (8th ed.). Routledge.
Cooper, J. (2011, December 5). Principals support state-wide staffing. *Education, 92*(12), 18.
Craft, J. (2015). Conceptualizing the policy work of partisan advisers. *Policy Sciences, 48*(2), 135–158. https://doi.org/10.1007/s11077-015-9212-2
Craft, J. (2016). *Backrooms and beyond: Partisan advisers and the politics of policy work in Canada*. University of Toronto Press.
Crawford, B. (2012, March 11). Principals to get greater say in how money spent under Adrian Piccoli's education shake-up in NSW. *Daily Telegraph*.
Datnow, A., Lasky, S. G., Stringfield, S. C., & Teddlie, C. (2005). Systemic integration for educational reform in racially and linguistically diverse contexts: A summary of the evidence. *Journal of Education for Students Placed At Risk, 10*(4), 441–453. https://doi.org/10.1207/s15327671espr1004_6
Dinham, S. (2012, March 19). Steep learning curve on path to more freedom. *Sydney Morning Herald*. https://www.smh.com.au/education/steep-learning-curve-on-path-to-more-freedom-20120318-1vdps.html
DiSalvo, D. (2017). Book Review of: The comparative politics of education: Teachers unions and educations systems around the world, by Terry M. Moe, Susanne Wiborg, Cambridge University Press, New York, NY, 2017, 344 pp. *Journal of School Choice, 11*(4), 663–665. https://doi.org/10.1080/15582159.2017.1395610
Dudley, S. (2023). *Politicians as policy makers in large-scale education system reform: The development of Local Schools, Local Decisions in NSW* [Doctoral dissertation]. UNSW Sydney.
Eacott, S., Niesche, R., Keddie, A., Blackmore, J., Wilkinson, J., Gobby, B., & MacDonald, K. (2022). Autonomy, instructional leadership and improving outcomes – the LSLD Reforms in NSW, Australia. *Leadership and Policy in Schools, 22*(3), 811–824. Retrieved 14 June, 2022, from https://doi.org/10.1080/15700763.2022.2081212

Earl, L., Watson, N., & Katz, S. (2003). *Large-scale education reform: Life cycles and implications for sustainability.* CfBT.

Edge, K (2015). Editorial. *Educational Assessment, Evaluation and Accountability, 27*(3), 201–203.

Edwards, M. (2021). Public policy process in Australia: Reflections from experience. In T. Mercer, R. Ayres, B. Head, & J. Wanna (Eds.), *Learning policy, doing policy: Interactions between public policy theory, practice and teaching* (pp. 165–184). ANU Press.

Edwards, M., Howard, C., & Miller, R. (2001). *Social policy, public policy: From problem to practice.* Routledge. https://doi.org/10.4324/9781003117254

Finnigan, K. S., & Daly, A. J. (2014). Conclusion: Using research evidence from the schoolhouse door to Capitol Hill. In K. S. Finnigan & A. J. Daly (Eds.), *Using research evidence in education: Policy implications of research in education, 2*. Springer. https://doi.org/10.1007/978-3-319-04690-7_1

Finnigan, K. S., Daly, A. J., & Che, J. (2013). Systemwide reform in districts under pressure. *Journal of Educational Administration, 51*(4), 476–497. https://doi.org/10.1108/09578231311325668

Fullan, M. (1991). *The new meaning of educational change.* Casel.

Fullan, M. (2010). *All systems go: The change imperative for whole system reform.* Corwin Press.

Fullan, M (2016b). The elusive nature of whole system improvement in education. *Journal of Educational Change, 17*(4), 539–544.

Fullan, M. (2016a). *The new meaning of educational change* (5th ed.). Teachers College Press.

Fullan, M., & Gallagher, M. J. (2020). *The devil is in the details: System solutions for equity, excellence and student well-being.* Corwin.

Fuller, K., & Stevenson, H. (2019). Global education reform: Understanding the movement. *Educational Review, 71*(1), 1–4. https://doi.org/10.1080/00131911.2019.1532718

Gale, T (2006). Towards a theory and practice of policy engagement: Higher education research policy in the making. *The Australian Educational Researcher, 33*(2), 1–14.

Gavin, M. (2019). *Changing conditions of work in neoliberal times: How the NSW Teachers' Federation has responded to changes in teachers' industrial and professional working conditions in NSW public education, 1985-2017* [Doctor of philosophy thesis]. The University of Sydney.

Gavin, M., Fitzgerald, S., & McGrath-Champ, S. (2022). From marketising to empowering: Evaluating union responses to devolutionary policies in education. *The Economic and Labour Relations Review, 33*(1), 80–99. https://doi.org/10.1177/10353046221077276

Gavin, M., & McGrath-Champ, S (2017). Devolving authority: The impact of giving public schools power to hire staff. *Asia Pacific Journal of Human Resources, 55*(2), 255–274.

Gavin, M. & Stacey, M. (2022). Enacting autonomy reform in schools: The re-shaping of roles and relationships under Local Schools, Local Decisions. *Journal of Educational Change.* Published online 21 April 2022. https://doi.org/10.1007/s10833-022-09455-5

Gift, T., & Wibbels, E. (2014). Reading, writing, and the regrettable status of education research in comparative politics. *Annual Review of Political Science, 17*(1), 291–312. http://www.annualreviews.org/doi/abs/10.1146/annurev-polisci-080911-131426

Gilding, L. (2021). The practical realities of policy on the run: A practitioner's response to academic policy frameworks. In T. Mercer, R. Ayres, B. Head, & J. Wanna (Eds.), *Learning policy, doing policy: Interactions between public policy theory, practice and teaching* (pp. 243–257). ANU Press.

Gillard, J. (2010, August 2). *Gillard Government gives power to parents and principals* [Press release].

Gillard, J. (2014). *My story.* (J. Gillard, Narr.) [Audiobook]. Bolinda Publishing Ltd.

Goldspink, C. (2007). Rethinking educational reform: A loosely coupled and complex systems perspective. *Educational Management Administration & Leadership, 35*(1), 27–50. https://doi.org/10.1177/1741143207068219

Griffin, D. (2013). *Education reform: The unwinding of intelligence and creativity*. Springer.

Hargreaves, A. (2007). Sustainable leadership and development in education: Creating the future, conserving the past. *European Journal of Education, 42*(2), 223–233.

Hargreaves, A. (2020). Large-scale assessments and their effects: The case of mid-stakes tests in Ontario. *Journal of Educational Change*. Published online 11 May 2020. https://doi.org/10.1007/s10833-020-09380-5

Hargreaves, A., & Fullan, M. (1998). *What's worth fighting for out there?* Teachers College Press.

Hargreaves, A., & Goodson, I (2006). Educational change over time? The sustainability and nonsustainability of three decades of secondary school change and continuity. *Educational Administration Quarterly, 42*(1), 3–41.

Hargreaves, A., & Shirley, D. (2009). *The fourth way: The inspiring future of educational change*. Corwin.

Hargreaves, A., & Shirley, D. (2012). *The global fourth way: The quest for educational excellence*. Corwin.

Harris, A., & Jones, M (2017). Leading educational change and improvement at scale: Some inconvenient truths about system performance. *International Journal of Leadership in Education, 20*(5), 632–641.

Hartley, J. (2010). Political leadership. In S. Brookes & K. Grint (Eds.), *The new public leadership challenge* (pp. 133–149). Palgrave MacMillan.

Hartley, K., Kuecker, G., & Woo, J. J. (2019). Practicing public policy in an age of disruption. *Policy Design and Practice, 2*(2), 163–181. https://doi.org/10.1080/25741292.2019.1622276

Hattersley, R. (2006, October 15). A bit of a wet Blunkett: David Blunkett's diaries reveal little new about cabinet life - but more than you need to know about him. *The Observer*, p. 23.

Hingston, J. I. (2018). *The impact of school autonomy reform on secondary principals* [Doctor of philosophy in education thesis]. The University of Newcastle.

Hollway, S. (1996). Departments and ministerial offices: an essential partnership. In J. Disney & J. R. Nethercote (Eds.), *The house on Capital Hill: Parliament, politics and power in the national capital* (pp. 133–148). Federation Press.

Hopkins, D., & Reynolds, D. (2001). The past, present, and future of school improvement: Towards the third age. *British Educational Research Journal, 27*, 459–475.

Hopkins, D., Stringfield, S., Harris, A., Stoll, L., & Mackay, T. (2014). School and system improvement: A narrative state of the art review. *School Effectiveness and School Improvement, 25*(2), 257–281.

Hoppe, R. (2018). Rules-of-thumb for problem-structuring policy design. *Policy Design and Practice, 1*(1), 12–29.

Hoy, W. K., & Miskel, C. G. (2012). *Educational administration: theory, research, and practice* (9th ed.). McGraw Hill.

Janmaat, J. G., Duru-Bellat, M., Green, A., & Mehaut, P. (Eds.). (2013). *The dynamics and social consequences of education systems*. Macmillan.

Kisby, B. (2011). Interpreting facts, verifying interpretations: Public policy, truth and evidence. *Public Policy and Administration, 26*(1), 107–127. https://doi.org/10.1177/0952076710375784

Lemke, J. L., & Sabelli, N. H. (2008). Complex systems and educational change: Towards a new research agenda. *Educational Philosophy and Theory, 40*(1), 118–129. https://doi.org/10.1111/j.1469-5812.2007.00401.x

Levin, B. (2007). Sustainable, large-scale education renewal. *Journal of Educational Change, 8*(4), 323–336.

Levin, B. (2008). *How to change 5000 schools: A practical and positive approach for leading change at every level*. Harvard Educational Press.

Levin, B. (2009). Does politics help or hinder education change? *Journal of Education Change, 10*, 69–72. https://doi.org/10.1007/s10833-008-9092-8

Levin, B. (2010). Governments and education reform: Some lessons from the last 50 years. *Journal of Education Policy, 25*(6), 739–747.

Levin, B., & Fullan, M. (2008). Learning about system renewal. *Educational Management Administration & Leadership, 36*(2), 289–303.

Lewin, K. (1943). Psychology and the process of group living. In M. Gold (Ed.), *The complete social scientist: A Kurt Lewin reader* (pp. 333–345). American Psychological Association. https://doi.org/10.1037/10319-015

Lingard, B. (2000). Federalism in schooling since the Karmel Report (1973), Schools in Australia: From modernist hope to postmodernist performativity. *The Australian Educational Researcher, 27*(2), 25–61. https://doi.org/10.1007/BF03219720

Lipscombe, B. (2011). New Minister. *Education, 92*(4), 16.

Louis-Seashore, K. (1998). 'A light feeling of chaos': Educational reform and policy in the United States. Daedalus.

Luetjens, J., Mintrom, M., & 't Hart, P. (Eds.). (2019). *Successful public policy: Lessons from Australia and New Zealand*. Australian National University Press.

Magni, F. (2013). *Adonis: Education, education, education: Reforming England's schools. Revista. Formazione, Lavoro, Persona, III* (9) (pp. 146–148). University of Bergamo.

Maley, M. (2015). The policy work of Australian political staff. *International Journal of Public Administration, 38*(1), 46–55.

McGrath-Champ, S., Stacey, M., Wilson, R., Fitzgerald, S., Rainnie, A., & Parding, K. (2019). Principals' support for teachers' working conditions in devolved school settings: Insights from two Australian States. *Educational Management Administration & Leadership, 47*(4), 590–605. https://doi.org/10.1177/1741143217745879

Mercer, T., Ayres, R., Head, B., & Wanna, J. (Eds.) (2021). *Learning policy, doing policy: Interactions between public policy theory, practice and teaching*. ANU Press.

Miller, N. (2002). Insider change leadership in schools. *International Journal of Leadership in Education, 5*(4), 343–360. https://doi.org/10.1080/13603120210141951

Mitchell, D. E., & Romero, L. (2018). *Politics of education*. Oxford University Press. https://doi.org/10.1093/OBO/9780199756810-0129

Moe, T. (2012). From the ballot to the blackboard: The redistributive political economy of education. *Perspectives on Politics, 10*(3), 846–847. https://doi.org/10.1017/S1537592712000837

Moe, T., & Wiborg, S. (Eds.) (2017). *The comparative politics of education: Teachers unions and education systems across the world*. Cambridge University Press.

Mourshed, M., Chijioke, C., & Barber, M. (2010). *How the world's most improved school systems keep getting better*. McKinsey & Co.

Moyson, S., Scholten, P., & Weible, C. M. (2017). Policy learning and policy change: Theorizing their relations from different perspectives. *Policy and Society, 36*(2), 161–177. https://doi.org/10.1080/14494035.2017.1331879

Mukherjee, I., & Bali, A. S. (2019). Policy effectiveness and capacity: Two sides of the design coin. *Policy Design and Practice, 2*(2), 103–114. https://doi.org/10.1080/25741292.2019.1632616

Mulheron, M. (2012, February 13). My new role teaching politicians. *Education, 93*(1), 20.

Mundy, K., Green, A., Lingard, B., & Verger, A. (2016). Introduction: The globalization of education policy – key approaches and debates. In K. Mundy, A. Green, B. Lingard, & A. Verger (Eds.), *The handbook of global education policy* (pp. 1–20). John Wiley & Sons.

Norman, M. (2006, October 13). The delusions and self-pity of David Blunkett. *The Independent*, p. 45.

NSW Department of Education. (2017). *Public submission made to the 'Review to Achieve Educational Excellence in Australian Schools'*. https://www.education.gov.au/system/files/documents/document-file/2020-12/nsw-department-of-education.docx

NSW Department of Education and Communities. (2011a). *Local schools, local decisions*. NSW Government.

NSW Department of Education and Communities. (2011b). *Local schools, local decisions: Discussion paper*. NSW Government.

NSW Department of Education and Communities. (2012a). *Local schools, local decisions: Report on the consultation*. NSW Government. https://schoolsequella.det.nsw.edu.au/file/3d9c0df5-e220-4e12-bc09-71a340d7126f/1/Local Decisions Report on Consultation_.pdf

NSW Department of Education and Communities. (2012b). *Final report of the evaluation of the school-based management pilot*. Student Administration and Program Evaluation Bureau. https://education.nsw.gov.au/content/dam/main-education/about-us/educational-data/cese/evaluation-evidence-bank/2012-school-based-management-pilot-evaluation.pdf

NSW Department of Education and Communities. (2012c). *Local schools, local decisions: Fact sheets*.

NSW Department of Education and Communities. (2012d). *Local schools, local decisions: Frequently asked questions*.

NSW Government. (2021). *Schools and students: 2021 statistical bulletin*, NSW Government. https://data.cese.nsw.gov.au/data/dataset/schools-and-students-statistical-bulletin

NSW Liberals & Nationals. (n.d.). *Local schools, local decisions: Plan to re-empower local school communities*.

NSW Liberals & Nationals. (2011). *Start the change; make NSW number one again*. Mark Needham.

NSW Secondary Principals' Council. (2011, November 18). *NSWSPC initial submission to Local Schools, Local Decisions consultation*.

NSW Teachers Federation. (2011, October 17). *Statement in response to Local Schools Local Decisions consultation*.

NSW Teachers Federation. (2011, November 4). *Federation rejects so-called 'independent evaluation' of the 47 schools pilot program*.

Nye, J. S. (1990). Soft Power. *Foreign Policy*, *80*, 153–171. https://doi.org/10.2307/1148580

O'Farrell, B. (2012, March 11). *Getting on with the job, honouring commitments: Local schools, local decisions* [Press release].

OECD. (2014). *Education at a glance 2014: OECD indicators*. OECD Publishing.

OECD. (2015). *Education policy outlook 2015: Making reforms happen*. OECD Publishing.

OECD. (2020). An implementation framework for effective change in schools. *OECD Education Policy Perspectives, No. 9*. OECD Publishing.

Peters, T. J., & Waterman, R. J. (1982). *In search of excellence: Lessons from America's best-run companies*. Harper & Row.

Peters, B. G., & Zittoun, P. (2016). *Contemporary approaches to public policy: Theories, controversies and perspectives*. Palgrave Macmillan.

Pétry, F. (2014). A tale of two perspectives: Election promises and government actions in Canada. In E. Gidengil & H. Bastedo (Eds.), *Canadian democracy from the ground up: Perceptions and performance* (pp. 231–252). UBC Press.

Piccoli, A. (2011, August 11). *Empowering local schools to enable better teaching and learning* [Press release].

Piccoli, A. (2013). Foreword. In D. E. Lynch & T. Yeigh (Eds.), *Teacher education in Australia: Investigations into programming, practicum and partnership* (pp. 11–15). Oxford Global Press.

Piccoli, A (2014). *Transforming education: The New South Wales reform journey*. London (Paper delivered at the Education World Forum, NSW Government, 21 January).

Pont, B. (2018). A comparative view of Education system reform: Policy, politics and people. In H.J. Malone, R-G Santiago, & K. Kew (Eds.), *Future directions of educational change: Social justice, professional capital, and systems change* (pp. 171–187). Routledge.

Risolia, W. (2015), cited in Bruns, B., Macdonald, I. H., & Schneider, B. R. (2019). The politics of quality reforms and the challenges for SDGs in education. *World Development*, *118*, 27–38. https://doi.org/10.1016/j.worlddev.2019.02.008

Rolheiser, C., Fullan, M., & Edge, K. (2002). Large-scale literacy reform. *Orbit*, *33*(1), 37–42.

Sahlberg, P. (2004). Teaching and globalization. *Managing Global Transitions*, *2*(1), 65–83.

Sahlberg, P. (2006). Education reform for raising economic competitiveness. *Journal of Educational Change*, *7*(4), 259–287. https://doi.org/10.1007/s10833-005-4884-6

Sahlberg, P. (2012). *Finnish lessons: What can the world learn from educational change in Finland?* Teachers College Press.

Sahlberg, P. (2016). The global education reform movement and its impact on schooling. In K. Mundy, A. Green, B. Lingard, & A. Verger (Eds.), *The handbook of global education policy* (pp.128–144). John Wiley and Sons Ltd.

Sarason, S. (1990). *The predictable failure of educational reform*. Jossey-Bass.

Savage, G. C. (2016). Who's steering the ship? National curriculum reform and the re-shaping of Australian federalism. *Journal of Education Policy*, *31*(6), 833–850.

Schleicher, A. (n.d). OECD Facebook. https://www.facebook.com/theOECD/posts/without-data-you-are-just-another-person-with-an-opinion-andreas-schleicher-crea/475315189147747/

Schneider, A. L., & Ingram, H. (1997). *Policy design for democracy*. University Press of Kansas.

Shergold, P. (2015). *Learning from failure: Why large government policy initiatives have gone so badly wrong in the past and how the chances of success in the future can be improved*. Australian Public Service Commission, Commonwealth of Australia.

Sherington, G., & Hughes, J. (2012). Education. In D. Clune & R. Smith (Eds.), *From Carr to Keneally: Labor in office in NSW 1995-2011* (pp. 138–49). Allen & Unwin.

Shrestha, U., Williams, T. P., Al-Samarrai, S., Van Geldermalsen, A., & Zaidi, A. (2019). What is the relationship between politics, education reforms, and learning? Evidence from a new database and nine case studies. *Background paper for World Development Report 2018: Learning to realize education's promise* (139 pp.). World Bank.

Smith, M. S., & O'Day, J. (1990). Systemic school reform. *Journal of Education Policy*, *5*(5), 233–267. https://doi.org/10.1080/02680939008549074

Smith, M., O'Day, J., & Fuhrman, S. (1992). State policy and systemic school reform. *Educational Technology*, *32*(11), 31–36. Retrieved March 4, 2021, from http://www.jstor.org/stable/44425489

Spillane, J. P. (2013). Diagnosing and designing for schoolhouse practice: Educational administration and instructional improvement. In H. J. Malone (Ed.), *Leading educational change: Global issues, challenges, and lessons on whole-system reform* (pp. 37–41). Teachers College Press.

Stacey, M (2017). The teacher 'problem': an analysis of the NSW education policy Great Teaching, Inspired Learning. *Discourse: Studies in the Cultural Politics of Education*, *38*(5), 782–793.

Stewart, R. G. (1999). *Public policy: Strategy and accountability*. Macmillan.

Supovitz, J. A., & Taylor, B. S. (2005). Systemic education evaluation: Evaluating the impact of systemwide reform in education. *American Journal of Evaluation*, *26* (2), 204–230. https://doi.org/10.1177/1098214005276286

Sydney Morning Herald. (2012, June 27). NSW teachers' strike upsets P&C. https://www.smh.com.au/national/nsw-teachers-strike-upsets-p-and-c-20120627-21159.html

Taflaga, M., & Kerby, M. (2020). Who does what work in a ministerial office: Politically appointed staff and the descriptive representation of women in Australian political offices, 1979–2010. *Political Studies, 68*(2), 463–485. https://doi.org/10.1177/0032321719853459

Teddlie, C., & Reynolds, D. (2000). *The international handbook of school effectiveness research.* Falmer Press.

Thomson, S., De Bortoli, L., Nicholas, M., Hillman, K., & Buckley, S. (2010). *Challenges for Australian education: Results from PISA 2009.* ACER.

Tiernan, A., & Weller, P. (2010). *Learning to be a minister: Heroic expectations, practical realities.* Melbourne University Press.

Verger, A (2014). Why do policy-makers adopt global education policies? Toward a research framework on the varying roles of ideas in education reform. *Issues in Comparative Education, 16*(2), 14–29.

Vinson, T., Esson, K., Johnston, K., & NSW Teachers Federation (2002). *Inquiry into the provision of public education in NSW: Report of the 'Vinson inquiry'.* Pluto Press.

Virani, A. (2019). Notions of policy effectiveness and implications for policy design: Insights from public-private partnerships in India. *Policy Design and Practice, 2*(2), 198–214. https://doi.org/10.1080/25741292.2019.1607812

Washington, S. (n.d.). What is the 'policy problem' and what's to be done about it? Building an infrastructure for great policy. *The Mandarin.* Retrieved October 31, 2019, from themandarin.com.au.

Washington, S., & Mintrom, M. (2018). Strengthening policy capability: New Zealand's policy project. *Policy Design and Practice 1*(1), 30–46. https://doi.org/10.1080/25741292.2018.1425086

Watson, S. L., Watson, W., & Reigeluth, C. M. (2008), Systems design for change in education and training. In J. M. Spector, M. D. Merrill, J. van Merrienboer, & M. P. Driscoll (Eds.), *Handbook of research for educational communications and technology* (3rd ed.) (pp. 691–701). Association for Educational Communication and Technology. Taylor & Francis.

West, P. (1991). Politics and education in NSW 1988-91: Management or human values? *Australian Educational Researcher, 18*(3), 53–67.

Whitty, G., Power, S., & Halpin, D. (1998). *Devolution and choice in education: The school, state, the market.* University Press

Wu, X., Ramesh, M., & Howlett, M. (2015). Policy capacity: A conceptual framework for understanding policy competences and capabilities. *Policy and Society, 34*(3–4), 165–171. https://doi.org/10.1016/j.polsoc.2015.09.001

Zadkovich, G. (2011, August 29). Behind the political rhetoric on devolved decision making. *Education, 92*(8), 1.

Zadkovich, G. (2011, October 24). Chance to influence devolution debate. *Education, 92*(10), 6.

Zadkovich, G. (2012, February 13). Major battle looms on staffing and devolution. *Education, 93*(1), 1.

Zeigler, L. H., & Johnson, K. F. (1972). *The politics of education in the states.* Bobbs-Merrill.

INDEX

Note: Locators in *italics* represent figures, locators in **bold** represent tables and locators followed by "n" refer to end notes.

Adonis, A. 21, 23n4, 58, 101–102, 116, 118, 120
Althaus, C. 20, 58, 77, 99, 101, 118, 124
Andrews, L. 21, 23n6, 58, 79, 99–101, 107, 110, 112, 118, 120, 122–124
Angus, M. 14
Australia 5, 8n4, 22–23, 29–31, 34, 40, 46, 72–73, 77, 86, 98, 100, 115
Australian Broadcasting Commission 70
Australian education system reform 28
Australian Ministerial Education Council 64
Australian Policy Cycle 101, 124
Ayres, R. 77, 118

Baker, K. 21, 23n3, 28
Ball, S. J. 12, 15, 37, 54, 56, 77, 98–99, 123–124, 127
Barber, M. 11, 18, 21, 79, 101, 114
Behm, A. 118
Better Schools 41–51, 53, 55–56, 59
Better Schools, Better Services (BSBS) 45–51, 54–55, 86
Birkland, T. A. 14, 37, 53, 55, 108
black box 3–8, 17, 105, 120
Blunkett, D. 21, 23n5, 100
Braun, V. 7, 105
Breakspear, S. 12–13
Bridgman, P. 21, 99, 111
Bruniges, M. 50, 59, 62–64, 80–81, 92, 111

Bruns, B. 4, 9, 16–17, 19, 35, 53, 55, 58, 75, 101–102, 107–110, 113, 117, 122, 128
Busemeyer, M. 4, 17, 35, 120

Caldwell, B. J. 14, 22, 28, 114
Campbell, C. 11–13, 122
Cane, C. 30, 41, 44, 50, 53, 56, 63–64, 81–83, 89–90, 94–95
Carr, B. 29
Carr, K. 32–33
Carter, D. 22, 116
Centre for Education Statistics and Evaluation (CESE) 7, 97–98, 115
Charter Letter 40–43, 46, 53–54
Christie, P. 41, 43–44, 57n1
Clarke, V. 7, 105
Cohen, D. K. 14, 18
Cohen, L. 19
Commonwealth of Australia 27
conducive environment 12
consultation process 30–33, 45–47, 50–51, 54, 57–60, 74–81, 84, 87–90, 93, 97, 99–102, 109–111, 114–115, 118, 124–125, 129; education stakeholders (*see* education stakeholders); politicians and government stakeholders 71–73
Cooper, J. 7, 33, 51, 64–66, 71, 88, 90, 94–95
Craft, J. 22

Index

Daly, A. J. 18
Datnow, A. 18
Davis, G. 21, 99, 111
decision-making ix, 6, 20, 32, 39, 42, 45–46, 58–59, 61, 68–69, 71, 73, 80, 82, 119–120, 128, 135
Department Liaison Officers (DLOs) 45, 47, 50, 53, 57n2, 64, 89, 94, 118
Dinham, S. 6, 114
DiSalvo, D. 58, 110
Dorothy Dixer 72, 78n6
Dudley, S. viii–xii

Earl, L. 10–14
educational system 4, 11, 16, 18, 20, 55
Education Authority 130–131
Education Ministers 4–6, 19, 21, 23, 28–30, 58, 60, 64, 87, 92, 94, 101, 105, 113, 115, 120, 123
Education Policy and Engagement System framework 127–129, *128*, 134
education reform 3, 6–7, 9–10, 12, 14, 18, 21, 35, 53, 56, 59, 68, 72, 108, 128, 135; agenda 29–33; political context of 15–17, 27–29
education stakeholders 5–6, 23, 30, 33, 37, 41–42, 47–49, 56, 59–72, 93–95, 117, 119, 126; engagement 109–110; principals' organisations 63–67; schools and principals 60–63; unions 67–71
Edwards, M. 15–16, 97, 100–101, 108, 118, 127
ERC/Treasury/Better Schools approach 55
evidence–based policy 114–115
evidence politics and policy 85–87
Expenditure Review Committee of Cabinet (ERC) 40, 42–44, 47, 49–50, 53–56, 72, 117

federal government 18, 72–74, 82, 107
Finnigan, K. S. 18
Flowerpot Nation 46–47, 51
47 Schools Pilot 29–30, 32, 72–74, 82, 86–87, 89, 102n1, 114
Fullan, M. viii, 4, 10–13, 18–19, 55

Gale, T. 118
Gallagher, M. J. 4, 11, 13
Gift, T. 57, 122
Gillard, J. 22, 23n8, 29–30, 58, 99, 101, 113, 118
Global Education Reform Movement (GERM virus) viii, 10, 16

Goldspink, C. 20, 36, 107, 127
Goodson, I. 35
Gove, M. 99
government: challenges for 4; goal 40–41; political context 80–81; in public policy making 14–15; stakeholders 71–73; in whole system improvement 3, 5, 9–23, 122–135, *131*
Greiner, N. 21, 28

Hargreaves, A. 10, 12, 35
Harris, A. 10, 13
Hartley, J. 122
Hartley, K. 15, 120
Hattersley, R. 21
Hawke, B. 23n11
Hayward, D. 22, 23n7
Hollway, S. 22, 23n11, 111
Hopkins, D. viii–x, xi, 4–5, 10–11, 13, 17–18, 122, 132
Hoppe, R. 4, 16, 108
Hoy, W. K. 18, 20
Hughes, J. 5, 29

inclusive stakeholder engagement 12
Ingram, H. 37
insiders and outsiders stakeholders 5, 7, 18–23, 74–75, 78, 93, 96, 107, 108, 128–129, 132, 134
International Congress for School Effectiveness and Improvement (ICSEI) xi

Johnson, K. F. 16
Jones, M. 10, 13

K-12 education 18
Kerby, M. 22
Kirk, K. 45–46
Kisby, B. 100
Klein, J. 30

Labor Government 28–29, 34, 72–73, 87
large-scale education system reform viii, ix, 3–15, 17–23, 28, 35, 53, 55–56, 75–77, 79, 83–84, 93–95, 98–102, 105, 109, 111, 113, 117, 119–120, 122–123, 125–126, 128–129, 132, 134
Lemke, J. L. 19, 75, 127
Levin, B. 4, 11
Lewin, K. 124
Lincoln, A. 67
Lingard, B. 28

Local Schools, Local Decisions (LSLD) ix, 6, 27, 32, 37, 39, 49, 51–52, 59, 66, 69, 81, 84, 86, 92–93; education stakeholders 93–95; fact sheets 90–91, *91*, 136, *137–141*; the Minister 96–97; policy announcement 80–81, 92–93; policy making process 105, **106**, 107
Louis-Seashore, K. 10
Luetjens, J. 15, 23, 98–99, 115

Mackay, A. ix
Magni, F. 21
Maley, M. 22
Marsh, M. 47–48, 50, 53, 64, 88–90, 94
Mercer, T. 77, 118, 122, 132, 135n1
Metherell, T. 21, 28
Miller, N. 18
Ministers: Diary Secretary 63; goal 39–42, 54; leadership role 6, 74, 76, 110, 119–120, 127, 129, 133; Office 5–6, 22–23, 42, 45–46, 48, 50–51, 53, 64–65, 72, 79, 81–83, 87–90, 92, 94–95, 99, 108, 111, 114, 118, 124, 127, 130–134; relationship with the department 110–112
Mintrom, M. 56, 98, 118, 120
Miskel, C. G. 18, 20
Mitchell, D. E. 15–16, 118
Moe, T. 16, 57–58, 122
Mourshed, M. 11, 46
Moyson, S. 14, 120
Mukherjee, I. 15, 120
Mularczyk, L. 33, 50, 61, 63–65, 81, 87–90, 93–96
Mulheron, M. 30, 33, 48, 66–70, 74, 88–90, 94–95

NAPLAN tests 31, 38n2
NSW Department of Education 5, 28–29, 33, 53, 86, 89–90, 117
NSW Department of Education and Communities 51, 55, 59, 81–82, 84, 86, 89–90
NSW education system reform 28–29
NSW Liberals & Nationals 32–33
NSW Minister for Education ix, 3, 5, 7, 29, 39, 56, 73, 79, 92, 99, 107, 116, 120, 130, 136
NSW Teachers Federation (NSWTF) 28–30, 32–33, 36, 48, 59, 64, 66–71, 73–74, 76, 84–85, 87–90, 92, 94, 99, 101, 102n2, 110, 117
NSWTF Principals' Conference 32
Nye, J. S. 57n3, 116

O'Day, J. 18
O'Farrell, B. 40, 92
open systems theory 19
Opposition Education Spokesperson 27, 108, 112, 117
Organisation for Economic Co-operation and Development (OECD) viii, 3–4, 10–12, 31, 132

Parents' and Citizens' Association 29, 66, 70
Peters, B. G. 37
Peters, T. J. 20
Pétry, F. 37
Piccoli, A. ix, xi, xii, 3, 5–7, 9, 22, 23n10, 27, 29–37, 39–41, 43, 45, 53–54, 58–59, 62, 65, 70, 73, 76, 79, 84, 88–89, 92–93, 96, 101, 105, 107–110, 112, 114–119, 122, 124
policy: actors 22, 129–134; capacity 14; centre 20, 36; dance 21, 99, 102, 111, 121, 129, 134; development process x, 4, 6–8, 12–14, 17, 22, 27, 35, 47, 51, 53–54, 56, 58, 77, 80–83, 85, 93, 97–99, 102, 105, 107–112, 114, 116, 118, 121, 123–135; as discourse 37, 54, 77, 99, 123; documents 88–92; makers ix, 3–10, 12–13, 15, 19, 35, 47, 53, 57, 77, 80–81, 93, 97, 99–100, 105–124, 126–127, 131–135; and politics 118–119; and system levers 84–85; as text 37, 54–55, 77, 80, 99, 123, 127, 129
policy-cycle approach 123
Policy Process Bow Tie framework 123–127, *125*, 134
political context 4–7, 15–17, 21–23, 27, 30, 35–36, 44–45, 47–48, 53–54, 56–58, 67, 71–75, 77–80, 96–97, 99, 102, 107–109, 116, 127, 129–130, 133–134
Pont, B. 35, 129
power and policy making 116–117, 127, 129–130
Primary Principals' Association (PPA) 51, 62, 66, 70, 94
Programme for International Student Assessment (PISA) viii, 3, 5, 10, 12–13, 31
public policy making 4, 6–8, 14–17, 20, 34–35, 37, 47, 53–56, 58, 77, 79–81, 83, 85, 97–100, 102, 107–108, 111, 115, 118–120, 122–123
Public Service Association (PSA) 59, 78n1

reform development 35, 41, 46, 54–55, 63, 65, 73, 77, 87, 94, 96, 105, 107–109, 117, 119, 123, 129–130, 133
research evidence 81, 114–115, 121, 130–131, 133
Resource Allocation Model (RAM) 85
Reynolds, D. 10, 17
Risolia, W. 113
Rolheiser, C. 10
Romero, L. 15–16, 118

Sabelli, N. H. 19, 75, 127
Sahlberg, P. viii, 9–10, 114
Sarason, S. 10
Savage, G. C. 28
Schneider, B. R. 4, 16–17, 35, 37, 53, 55, 58, 75, 101–102, 108–110, 113, 122
school principal 112–113
Secondary Principals' Council (SPC) 30, 61, 65–66, 93, 113
Shergold, P. 54, 57n4, 97–99, 111–112, 115, 119
Sherington, G. 5, 29
Shirley, D. 10
Shrestha, U. 35, 40, 46, 55–56, 58, 100–101, 110, 115–116, 118–119, 122
Smartbuy 32
Smarter Schools National Partnership 29, 72, 82, 87
smart policy 12
Smith, M. 17–18
soft power 49, 53, 55–56, 116–117, 130
Spillane, J. P. 6, 12, 77, 123–124
Staffing Agreement 84–85
stakeholders 30–35; education (*see* education stakeholders); insiders and outsiders 5, 7, 18–23, 74–75, 78, 93, 96, 107, 108, 128–129, 132, 134; politicians and government 71–73; triangulation with 87–88

State Government 28–29, 71–73
steering policy 22
Stewart, R. G. 56, 98
Supovitz, J. A. 10, 18
systemic reform 4, 14, 18, 115

Taflaga, M. 22
Taylor, B. S. 10, 18
Teddlie, C. 10
Ten Guiding Principles 133, 135
three Ps (policy, politics, and people) 129–130
Tiernan, A. 21–22, 93
Trampusch, C. 4, 17, 35, 120
Treasury 42–44

Verger, A. 53
Vinson, T. 29
Virani, A. 4, 14, 108

Washington, S. 56, 98, 118, 120
Waterman, R. J. 20
Watson, S. L. 18
Weller, P. 21–22, 93
Welsh education sector 21
West, P. 21, 28
The West Wing (TV series) 7, 8n8
Whitlam, Gough 28
Whitty, G. 14
whole system improvement 3, 5, 9–23, 122–135, *131*
Whole System Reform Policy Development framework 129–132, *131*, 134
Wibbels, E. 57, 122
Wiborg, S. 16, 57–58
Wu, X. 14–15, 120

Zadkovich, G. 68–69
Zeigler, L. H. 16
Zittoun, P. 37